Safe in My Father's Arms

YOU CAN FORGIVE THE UNFORGIVABLE

Safe in My Father's Arms

LISE-MARIE LANGILLE

PLATYPUS
PUBLISHING

ISBN: Although the author and publisher have made every effort to ensure that the information in this book was correct at press time, the author and publisher do not assume and hereby disclaim any liability to any party for any loss, damage, or disruption caused by errors or omissions, whether such errors or omissions result from negligence, accident, or any other cause.

Copyright © 2023 Lise-Marie Langille

All rights reserved.

ISBN: 978-1-962133-11-1

DEDICATION

I dedicate this book to all those who have been hurt, not just the ordinary hurts of life, but those that surpass the imagination. When you are courageous enough to face life's hurt, when you face the truth, you will be set free. Take one step at a time, forgive, and know that the hurt will no longer bind you to bitterness and resentment. You can begin a new chapter; one where you can be all you can be, as you love and freely forgive as hurts come your way, one hurt at a time. Exercise your forgiveness muscles; live a life cleansed from the poison of an unforgiving heart and let your light shine!

Thank you Lord for setting my soul free!

CONTENTS

ACKNOWLEDGEMENTS		ix
INTRODUCTION		x
1.	THE HURT	1
2.	PEACEFUL PLACE	11
3.	THE LETTERS	21
4.	HEALING	29
5.	THE TRUTH	41
6.	BETRAYAL	51
7.	Go! FEAR NOT	59
8.	EXERCISE AND SOCIALIZE	71
9.	PEACE AND PURPOSE	79
10.	LOVING YOURSELF AND OTHERS	89
11.	TRIGGERS THAT CAUSE US TO FALL	99
12.	PROMISES ARE YES IN CHRIST	107
	RESOURCES	113

ACKNOWLEDGEMENTS

Thank you to my brother, Chris, and friends Fern, Karen, and Sonya for their dedication in reading the companion journal as well as each chapter in this book, thoroughly editing, and giving suggestions. You encouraged me, and I feel blessed that you were a part of my journey in writing my first Christian book.

Thank you to my husband Todd and my dear friend Thomas for your encouraging words and to everyone who offered any insight from a reader's perspective.

Thank you from the bottom of my heart.

INTRODUCTION

Welcome to "*Safe In My Father's Arms,*" YOU CAN FORGIVE THE UNFORGIVABLE. This 14-step forgiveness journey goes along with the workbook "*Safe In My Father's Arms Forgiveness Journal*".

Life is not easy and if you have picked up this book you are probably hurting from past events, or hurting in your present circumstance. I know what you are going through and wish I could be sitting beside you holding your hand letting you know you will get through this hurt. It will take time because forgiveness is not easy when we have been wronged.

I am here to tell you that there is a way to obtain peace, a peace that surpasses all understanding. Like you, I chose to live in a state of bitterness and resentment with a protective heart, a heart that does not easily trust or forgive. But I was struggling, my wounded heart needed healing. It was only when I surrendered my circumstances over to the loving arms of my Heavenly Father that I started to experience a sense of peace and purpose.

I know firsthand what it is like to go day after day, month after month, and year after year holding on to hurts that were meant to be released. I witnessed the hurt I was causing others with my unforgiving heart. I woke up one morning after a terrible incident that changed my life and, it caused a built-in fear that I could not shake.

After months of being a victim of my circumstance, I took my first steps toward healing by daily walking with women in my neighbourhood. On a walk with God, I poured my heart and soul out to him asking him to release me from the pain I was enduring. He took my hand and guided me through each of the pages of this book. He took me on a 30-day journey of personal transformation.

I am still recovering, and each day I witness God's hand in every facet of my life, with my spouse, family, and others. I pray this book will give you a small glimpse of the amazing power of our Lord Jesus Christ and his ability to take a traumatic event and turn it into beauty. Christ changed my life. He can change yours. Walk to your Heavenly Father's loving arms. He is waiting for you.

CHAPTER 1 THE HURT

Jesus said, "Father, forgive them, for they do not know what they are doing." And they divided up his clothes by casting lots. -- Luke 23:34 (NIV)

We can only imagine the anguish Jesus felt when he was nailed to the cross and allowed to suffer hour by hour, the pain, so great and mistreatment so inhumane. I bring myself back to Jesus on the cross when I wake up to start my day and I remember hurt from my past but none that would ever compare to the suffering our Lord Jesus bared on the cross. The vision of the cross through each hurt showed me the sin I suffered from others but also the hurt I have caused others.

You have opened this book and my prayer is you are ready to face your hurts. You are hurting or just getting through a hurt; you have decided once and for all to get rid of any bitterness or anger from the event. It took months maybe even years to get to this step. You should be very proud of yourself; I have to admit it was easier to be bitter and alone in my hurt. Deep down in my heart, I knew I couldn't stay in this place for long. I could see the hurt I was causing to those I loved; I was wounded. I had to face the fact that I was hurting and sometimes unintentionally hurt others. No one could tell me it was time. I knew I did not want to spend any more time in this place. Today let's begin by curling up under a warm cozy blanket with our Bibles reading, **Be kind and compassionate to one another, forgiving each other, just as in Christ God forgave you. -- Ephesians 4:32 (NIV)**

Like me, you have probably tried every other option. You have cried, you have chatted with close friends and relatives but nothing is taking the pain away. You want it to go away once and for all because you have tried in your own strength but the pain just seems to be festering. It is now starting to control your thoughts; it is controlling your relationships and your friendships. You might even be thinking "Doesn't anyone see my pain? Don't you understand? It isn't as easy to forget and move on? I am a victim and I am suffering? Just because you can't see my pain because I am acting so strong doesn't mean it isn't still there."

Trust me, your loved ones see your pain because you have changed but they are probably hoping and praying you will get through this event like you have gotten through many other hurtful times in your life. They just don't know what to say or do. They are not equipped to help you in your trauma event. I know with my situation counselors were not equipped to assist us. They openly admitted to my husband and I that they had never had a case like ours before. We felt very much alone. We needed to trust only in God and realize God was there in our hurt and we needed to draw on His strength to get through this terrible event.

In my pain, I exhausted my friends and family with my bitterness and unforgiving heart for months. I didn't want to leave my house I was perfectly fine to stay in the safety net of my home. Covid struck at the perfect time because it was my excuse when I didn't feel like facing the world. It was a wonderful excuse that allowed me to maintain my present state of seclusion and hurt.

I would occasionally leave my house to go for a walk with women in my neighbourhood. This was my opportunity to act like my life was normal and all was fine. Boy! Who was I kidding? I did this for months. I became quite the actress until I couldn't act any more.

Small hurts or large hurts, hurts of any size have an impact on the person we are today. And if I was perfectly honest, the trauma event changed my life and who I was becoming. Compound this with past hurts and you have a recipe that screams bitterness, mistrust and fear. You may be going through other hurts not as extreme as someone trying to harm you, but whatever the case, any hurt if left to fester in your heart will lead to building walls and bitterness will take over. Let's take for instance that you may be subject to being bullied at your work place or school. One or two people are making your life miserable and even though you have tried to turn the other cheek, it still leaves after- effects and scars. Or you may be living with a controlling spouse that tears you down rather than builds you up and you are doing all you can to build your own positive self esteem. But it can be pretty hard to stay in an environment of abuse without feeling the effects.

I want you to know whatever your present circumstances are, you are not alone, and God is there through all hurts big or small. Just recently a personal friend said something that hurt me. It would be what I would define as a small hurt. Sometimes our feelings might get hurt more easily than other times and at present I am more delicate in this area than I ever have been before. If you are anything like me, during sensitive patches in life you might have a tendency to ruminate, over think, dwell on every word allowing a person to control your thoughts. This is not what God wants you to believe about your present circumstance and you need to bring the thought to him.

Like most people, I allow a comment to fill my head with doubt, and I start questioning my abilities. I allow my mind to think maybe I shouldn't write this book after all; maybe no one is in need of healing like I am. Have you ever gone down that bunny trail; the bunny trail of self pity that God never intended you to go down?

Sure it hurts and we have to acknowledge it for what it was, a hurt. I had to define what a small hurt is so I could get a clearer understanding of what was going through my head. Hopefully it will be helpful to you too so when you encounter obstacles such as these you too will be able to name it. Well to begin, a hurt usually first penetrates on our heart. It affects our thoughts; it sometimes controls our ability to persevere if we allow it to. A word spoken can actually paralyze the receiver and cause them to question their capabilities and even their walk. When put in perspective, each time a hurt occurred I had to realize I was giving someone else power over my thoughts about me. That is not where God wants us to be. So I hung up the phone and I wrestled with the conversation I was having with my friend, partly because this was a person I trusted. Of course this person did not want to hurt me and probably had no idea that her words hurt. So I had to put it into perspective not allowing the enemy to get a foothold on my thoughts. If left unchecked these thoughts would keep me captive and start controlling my day and how it would unfold. When you are on a healing journey it is important not to allow negative thoughts to enter your head.

I was reminded yesterday by the speaker at our church that our lives are filled with social media to the extent of allowing it to consume our minds. I was actually thankful when he spoke about Facebook that I am not a part of that life. It made so much sense what he was saying. Each day if we look at social media we are allowing the world to dictate our feelings. If our friend posts a gathering and we are not invited we automatically are hurt. What do we do with that hurt? Do we tell the person or harbor resentment and build walls to communication?

We have a choice, we can allow others to dictate who we are or we can choose to place God as the one who directs our path and also defines who we are under His loving arms of acceptance. I don't know about you but I don't need to have anyone else place a mark on my life.

The list of people who hurt me has influenced my life enough and it is time for me to let that go and let God deal with them in His way. He loves them too but he does not want us to harbor bitterness and resentment.

God wants our thoughts and His will to be done. Scripture states,

We demolish arguments and every pretension that sets us up against the knowledge of God, and we take captive every thought to make it obedient to Christ. -- 2 Corinthians 10:5 (NIV)

We daily need to do this. What can we do to give our minds over to the Lord's control? One of the most important steps on our forgiveness and healing journey is keeping our thoughts captive to the obedience of Christ, being in constant prayer, meditating on his word and listening to God's guidance.

Once we come to the realization that it is his purpose we are to focus on, all the other comments won't bother us so much. He will always be our safe place to fall. Safety is in His arms and I needed to rely on him and him alone. He and only He will give us the courage and the discernment to do any task; writing for His purpose was what He has called me to do. I am not sure what He is calling you to do in your present hurt; I am so happy that I am going to be walking along side you in your hurt but remember my steps do not trump God's steps in your walk.

I needed to go to God daily and talk with Him and allow Him to heal my wounds. It wasn't until I faced this fact, that humans are not equipped to help me, only God, that I could begin my journey to healing. He will definitely place people in your life to walk alongside you but they are only there to encourage you. If they are not encouraging you, you need to pray He places uplifting people in your life to help you on your journey to healing.

In every hurtful situation on my journey to healing I had to pick myself up, dust the hurt off my shoulders and start to think about the hurt. This brought me to the vision of the cross and our Lord Jesus Christ. Every time we sin or someone sins against us, it hurts him and I pictured another nail on his cross. That is how my healing journey began. I saw the cross and the nails representing every hurt that occurred in my lifetime starting from the bottom hurts from my past all the way to the largest hurt, the hurt that I was facing last year when I was harmed. I drew a cross and a nail for every hurt starting from the bottom to the top.

This is what God brought to mind as I walked with him on a day I was hurting and crying out to him. I went home and immediately took a piece of paper out, drew a cross and started at the bottom placing a nail and the hurtful incident and moved my way up the cross to the most significant incident.

This first step is a huge step and you should be very proud of yourself to be vulnerable and honest about all the hurts in your life. After you complete the steps at the end of the chapter, I want you to picture the page, the people, and the events and in your mind draw a heart around all the hurts. The picture is what your heart feels every day of your life until you once and for all can remove those hurts from the page.

Eventually, I pray that over time your page will be empty. Not that you won't have hurt like you do today but you will deal with the hurt as it happens in your life because you will face it, write the hurt and either burn the hurt or send the hurt. This step will be explained in greater detail later on. One way or another the hurt will be dealt with as it comes; this is much healthier than harboring hurt and not dealing with the emotions that surround it. That is a recipe for bitterness and anger to take root in your heart and the walls will begin to form.

As much as we would like to think we have handled the hurt and moved on from it, if we do not deal with the hurt it will fester and affect our relationships. True freedom begins when we can freely let go of resentment towards another person. That is living a life

God intended and not being controlled by the circumstances that surround us.

Sometimes when I write these words I look back and say I don't want you to think I have overcome this journey. Not at all! I have a heart that does not forgive people easily so God wants me to be free of this unforgiving heart. He wants the same for you too.

Just remember this is a journey so don't get discouraged if you need to go back to the cross and place the same people there; our goal is to freely forgive as hurts come our way.

Now, this is in no way suggesting that you should allow hurts such as abuse to be happening over and over in your life. I am not a counselor but would definitely suggest that you make an appointment to see one in areas where you can potentially be in danger. God is not calling us to stay in dangerous situations. I would strongly recommend you seek counseling if you in any way feel unsafe in the environment you are living.

I encourage you that before you begin this journey that you pray out to God asking him to reveal any and all of the hurts from when you were very young to your present day. You will find that God will reveal each incident and the pain and hurt it caused. You will need this paper later on as you go through your healing journey. I am so proud that you are willing to take this step of healing and have realized that you are not alone. There are so many struggling with past hurts and some may not even realize how the hurt has taken captive in their lives to the point they are being held hostage by bitterness and a heart that continues to harden. Have you ever had the following thoughts with every hurt you face daily: *"The world is unsafe. I will never heal. I am a victim. I will always fear. I can never truly forgive. I am not worthy to be used by God. What is wrong with me? Why me? They don't deserve my forgiveness."*

These are the thoughts that keep us captive. The enemy wants to keep you in this captive state.

You can break the chains that bind you from an unforgiving heart and be set free. Come to your Heavenly Father's arms and allow him to heal your wounds so you can be once and for all set free and move from victim to victor in Christ. I am so looking forward to our journey to healing and forgiveness.

Let's pray:

Heavenly Father we come to you today in tears as we look over the wounds that have kept us captive in being all we can be for you. We ask you to bring to mind all the hurts we have not dealt with big or small. Allow us to be real before you with all our emotions; anger, bitterness, shame, and resentment. We know you and only you can release us from the hurt and the bitterness we carry from an unforgiving heart. We ask for healing in Jesus name we pray. Amen.

Reflections and steps to complete:

Step 1: Being vulnerable in writing out your hurts (privately in prayer)

1) Spend time in prayer asking God to reveal the past and present hurts you faced in your lifetime.

2) On a piece of paper list the hurts.

3) Beside each hurt name the person who hurt you.

Step 2: Placing the hurts on the cross (privately in prayer)

1) Use the cross in this book or draw a larger one and print the names of the people who hurt you, smallest hurt at the bottom of the cross to largest hurt the top nail on the cross.

Group discussion or personal reflection

You may want to share your answer within a bible study or small group.

After reading the bible verses in this chapter, which verse spoke to you the most and did it assist you with your hurt?

1) Jesus said, "Father, forgive them, for they do not know what they are doing." And they divided up his clothes by casting lots. -- Luke 23:34 (NIV)

2) Be kind and compassionate to one another, forgiving each other, just as in Christ God forgave you. -- Ephesians 4:32 (NIV)

3) We demolish arguments and every pretension that sets us up against the knowledge of God, and we take captive every thought to make it obedient to Christ. -- 2 Corinthians 10:5 (NIV)

You have now just completed the first and second step in healing the hurts in your life. You should be very proud of yourself. Well done! You may want to share this list with a trusted friend or counselor.

The Hurt

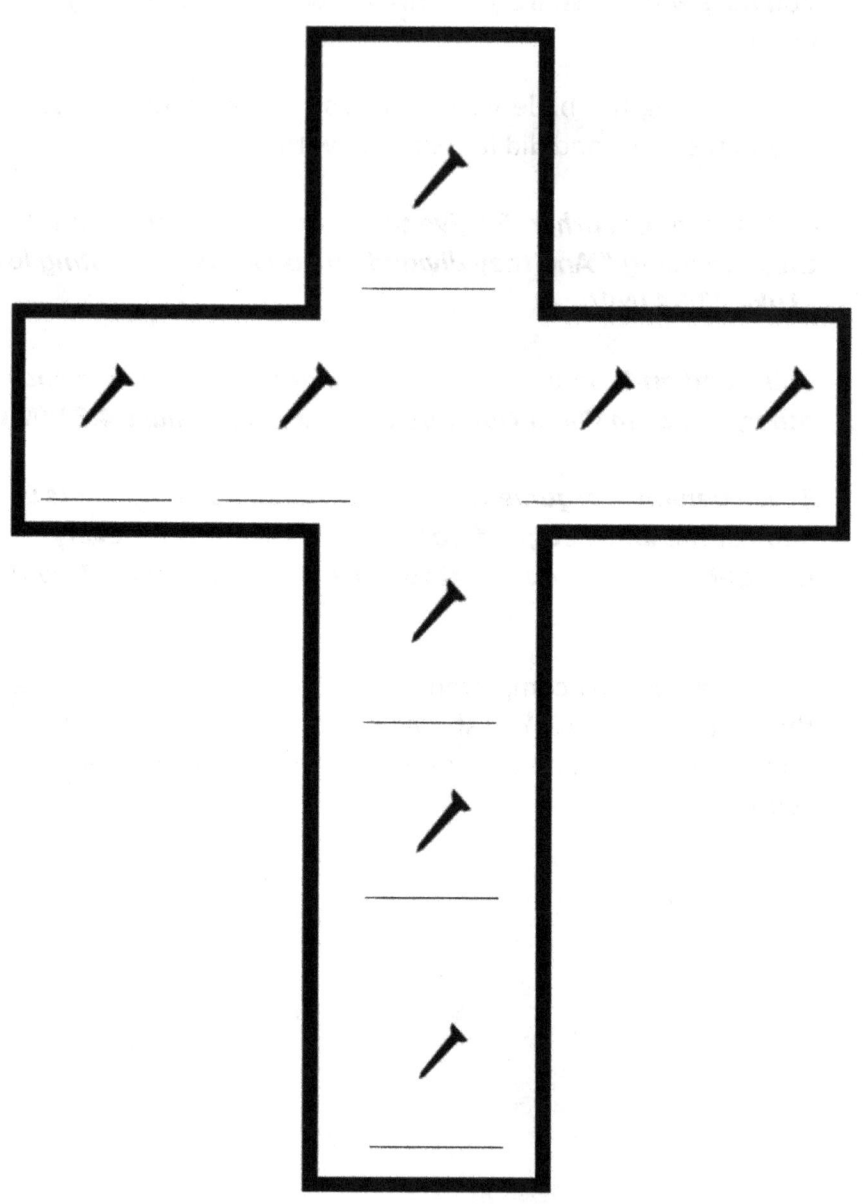

CHAPTER 2 PEACEFUL PLACE

Very early in the morning, while it was still dark, Jesus got up, left the house and went off to a solitary place, where he prayed.—Mark 1:35 (NIV)

You have now completed steps one and two in Chapter one. Before we go deeper into writing letters, I think it is important to find a warm, cozy, peaceful place you can call your own.

This peaceful place can be a closet as it is in my home or a second bedroom that you feel will provide solitude. Whatever place you select, pray first for God to direct you to this peaceful place. Select the perfect time and place for you to meditate and pray; where there are no distractions or noise. Don't worry if you don't feel an immediate prompting; try to choose a space wherever you feel comfortable to read the bible and write your thoughts. Be sure to have a place for your Bible and notes. You may want a binder with loose-leaf and plain paper to journal and draw pictures. If you purchased the accompanying journal to go along with the book you can just have that on the table with your Bible.

Fortunately, we own a house with two bedrooms upstairs; God gave me a vision long ago of the closet upstairs being my prayer room. Both bedrooms upstairs have their own two separate closets. After watching the movie "Prayer Room" years ago, I was reminded of the importance of uninterrupted prayer time with God. One of my girlfriends and I started going deeper into our faith by reading Christian books and having book studies every Friday morning from 7:30 a.m to 8:30 a.m. She was like my accountability partner. We read a chapter and share on Friday mornings; we have wonderful fellowship, and we have continued this for years and still do it today.

Before I watched the movie "Prayer Room" and while I was raising my children I always felt that I had to go away to a retreat to be close to God. I found my special Christian retreat called "Inthestillness Retreat" in St. Martins, NB, Canada. I want you to read the following words I wrote to describe this place of peaceful solitude:

Inthestillness Retreat is nestled on top of the woods overlooking the Bay of Fundy. If one needs to be in touch with God and find answers to unanswered questions, this is a wonderful place to meditate and pray. The log cabin is humbly set in the woods, with its warmth of character but the simplicity of articles; no TV, computer, radio, or electronics; just a bed, couch, firewood, kitchenette, and whirlpool bath. The most beautiful scenery of the Bay of Fundy, Brown's Beach, and rugged red rocks can be witnessed through a large picturesque window. In complete solitude, there is no sound but the ticking of a clock, and the image way in the distance of silent waves crashing against the rocks; peace, security, and time to meditate with God.

Do you notice in the description above that there are no distractions in this peaceful place in the woods? However, when you set up your place don't feel it has to be a place far away. Someone who has little children may feel they need to go on a retreat, but your retreat can be a basement or closet you set up. The one thing you will probably have difficulty finding is solitude and alone time. The time of day you select can be when the children are sleeping or early in the morning before they wake. I remember getting up before my children, so I could kick start my day with prayer.

Today it is just my husband and me; I have a prayer room and he is walking alongside me on this forgiveness journey. He mentioned we could use the same closet but I was quick to say no. I truly believe a person needs their own prayer space. I looked at the other spare bedroom with its two closets and thought one of them would be perfect for his prayer room. I cleaned it out, or should I say moved the items to the adjacent closet, washed the walls, photocopied the journal, and placed the pages in a binder for him, next to his Bible on a desk. You will find more success if you create a dedicated space that allows you to be alone with God.

I drove to the Great Canadian Dollar Store and purchased a corkboard and tacks for the two of us. I think it came to roughly five dollars each; placed a nail in the wall in each of our prayer rooms and hung the corkboards above the desks. Yours may be on the wall space you expose when pushing clothes hangers aside. I cut the cross out that has the nails on it from my journal and tacked it to each of the boards as a visual reminder for us of the people we needed to forgive. I placed the Day One 30-day Forgiveness/Healing Journal Challenge from the journal on the corkboards along with copies of the Bible verses at the back of the journal that we could check off each day as we completed our challenge toward forgiveness. Once created, we have our place to meditate and pray to go through the forgiveness and healing journey, as well as have alone time with God.

My husband and I could have used the same prayer room, but we both like having our own prayer space. I don't go in his prayer room closet and he doesn't go in mine, not because we couldn't, but it is now our safe place that provides us time alone with God and it is accessible whenever we choose to enter our sanctuary.

We started out doing our prayer time at different times of the day. I would complete my journal reading and writing in the morning and he would do his forgiveness journal after he took his bath at night. I am finding now I read my devotional in the morning and either go for my alone walk with God or walk with the women in the neighborhood and then write. So my journal time is now in the evenings at the same time as my husband's.

Establishing a routine will help you find peace with the time you spend with God by allowing you to fit it into your daily schedule. Someone mentioned, "Does it matter if a person spends time with God while folding clothes or watching TV?" Not at all! For instance, I would never say no to a chat with God while driving the car or anytime during the day. But I would suggest a solitary place away from distractions if you are going to commit to the forgiveness and healing journey, even if this means getting up an hour before going to work or shutting the TV down an hour before you head to bed.

I do hope you find this personal prayer space so you can go to this little retreat daily and spend some time alone with God as you journey through your forgiveness and healing.

Let's pray:
Heavenly Father, Thank you for showing me this peaceful place where I can feel your presence; safely wrapped in your loving arms knowing the Holy Spirit is deepening my connection with you. I want to be all I can be for you and know there are areas in my life that I have fallen short and I ask you to bring to my mind any areas of my life that are not pleasing in your eyes. I look at the cross with my name printed below and pray that you will show me the areas I need to place before you so I can forgive myself for my shortcomings and move on in my forgiveness and healing journey. Amen

My prayer is once you have completed the step below and have forgiven yourself, you will see yourself through the lens of God. He is your comforter who will bring you to a deeper understanding of who you are in Christ. Finding this new identity, the person we are in Christ, is like having a new set of lenses; having a sense of inner peace of who you are supposed to be on earth. In this peaceful place, there may be hurts that brings negative thoughts to your mind. However, focus on the Lord so you can see yourself through His eyes. You are going to be real before Him with all your flaws, and forgive yourself for your shortcomings. God has forgiven you and his loving arms are waiting to comfort you.

Reflection and steps to complete

Step 3: Peaceful Place

1) Set up your cozy place. Decide where and when you will pray daily?

2) Cut out all the Bible verses in your Forgiveness Journal workbook on pg 72-74 or write down the bible verses at the beginning of each chapter and any favorite verses on sticky note. Place these verses in your prayer room for you to read daily.

3) Listen to God's still, small voice. Turn to **Psalm 139** and find a verse to meditate on. Read it over and over and ask God who you need to add to your Hurt list.

4) What are the areas in your life that are hindering your walk with God? For the beginning of your journey, sit in your cozy prayer spot and draw a cross or use the cross at the end of this chapter. When I started this journey to forgiveness I realized I had areas of my life where I had to forgive myself first, before I started my journey of forgiving others. When I was going through my journal and read **Psalm 139,** God showed me my flaws that I needed to place on the cross. At the bottom of the cross, I put my name and all the areas in my life that hinder my walk with Christ. Use the cross on page 18 and allow God to bring to mind areas you need to work on in your life. **Is there hidden jealousy, anger, harsh speech, worry, shame, etc?**

Group discussion or personal reflection

You may want to share your answer within a Bible study or small group.

After reading the Bible verses in this chapter, consider which verse(s) spoke to you the most about finding a peaceful place, as well as assisted you in your step in forgiving yourself?

1) Very early in the morning, while it was still dark, Jesus got up, left the house and went off to a solitary place, where he prayed.-- Mark 1:35 (NIV)

2) "Be still and know that I am God; I will be exalted among the nations, I will be exalted in the earth."Psalm 46:10 (NIV)

3) *O Lord, you have searched me,*
and you know me.
You know when I sit and when I rise;
you perceive my thoughts from afar.
You discern my going out and my lying down;
you are familiar with all my ways.
Before a word is on my tongue
you know it completely, O Lord.
You hem me in -behind and before;
you lay your hand upon me.
Such knowledge is too wonderful for me,
too lofty for me to attain.
Where can I go from your Spirit?
Where can I flee from your presence?
If I go up to the heavens, you are there;
if I make my bed in the depths, you are there.
If I rise on the wings of the dawn,
if I settle on the far side of the sea,
even there your hand will guide me,
your right hand will hold me fast.
If I say, "Surely the darkness will hide me
and the light become night around me,"
even the darkness will not be dark to you;
the night will shine like the day,
for darkness is as light to you.
For you created my inmost being;
you knit me together in my mother's womb.
I praise you because I am fearfully and wonderfully made;
your works are wonderful,
I know that full well.

*My frame was not hidden from you
when I was made in the secret place,
when I was woven together in the depths of the earth.
Your eyes saw my unformed body;
all the days ordained for me were written in your book
before one of them came to be.
How precious to me are your thoughts, O God!
How vast is the sum of them!
Were I to count them,
they would outnumber the grains of sand
when I awake, I am still with you.
If only you would slay the wicked, O God!
Away from me, you bloodthirsty men!
They speak of you with evil intent;
your adversaries misuse your name.
Do I not hate those who hate you, LORD,
and abhor those who rise up against you?
I have nothing but hatred for them;
I count them my enemies.
Search me, O God, and know my heart;
test me and know my anxious thoughts.
See if there is any offensive way in me,
and lead me in the way everlasting. Psalm 139 (NIV)*

You have now just completed the third step in your forgiveness and healing journey. You should be very proud of yourself. Well done! You may want to share areas in your life you will be working on overcoming with a trusted friend, spouse, or counselor.

Peaceful Place

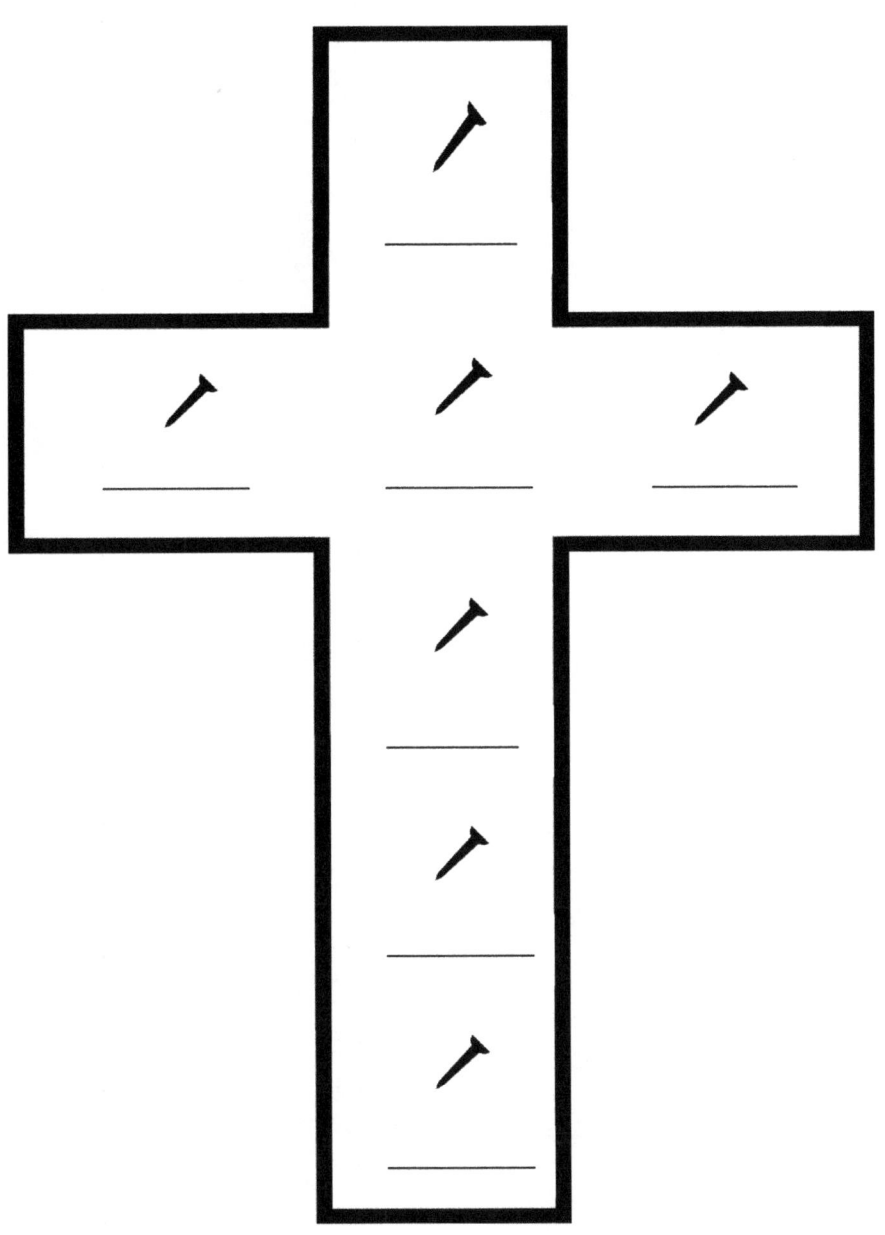

STAY IN PRAYER DURING THIS TIME OF HEALING

CHAPTER 3 THE LETTERS

"Why do you look at the speck of sawdust in your brother's eye and pay no attention to the plank in your own eye?"
Mathew 7:3 (NIV)

You have completed steps one through three and are ready to write letters; this is step four and five in your forgiveness and healing journey. I would like you to find your cross with all the hurts in your life. You are going to look at the bottom hurt. It may look like a small hurt, but all hurt has an impact on our lives. If you have not cut out your cross of hurts, you might like to place it on the wall of your peaceful room. You will be going to your cross daily and checking off the hurts as God calls you to deal with each one.

My journey to forgiveness started with an honest talk with God about all the people on my list of hurts. I cried many tears over the hurts and the people listed on my cross of hurts. I knew God was calling me not to rush this step. I wrote my first letter and I was emotionally overwhelmed by what God revealed to me. Believe it or not, I was the first person on my cross; I had to forgive myself for the hurt I caused others. I wrote my letters to the people and the Holy Spirit overwhelmed me with the hurts and to whom I needed to write letters.

Even though I placed myself first at the bottom of the cross of what I thought was a small hurt, it was a huge hurt in my life but also a big hurt in the lives of my children. It was the breakdown of a marriage that ended in divorce. The reason my name was on my cross was I had never truly forgiven myself for the part I played in the divorce. Interesting how we can always see the flaws of other people at the time of the event, but never those of ourselves.

The Bible verse that comes to mind is, **"Why do you look at the speck of sawdust in your brother's eye and pay no attention to the plank in your own eye?" Mathew 7:3 (NIV)**.God brought to mind when I searched my own heart that I had to ask for forgiveness from my children for the part I played in the divorce. This was such a difficult step. I wrote my first letter to God asking for forgiveness, but then was prompted to write to each of my children.

I found the first nail the most draining. I cried and was emotional for days. I wrestled with God for days about whether I was to burn the letter or send the letter to my children. I think hurts are easy to write down if they are private to us, but God was not allowing me to heal from this hurt. I knew the only way I was going to properly heal was to send the letters to each of my children.

If you are wrestling with what God is asking you to do, wait and keep the letter and just pray over the next couple of days. I found reading the Bible and daily devotionals helpful during this time of healing.

Nevertheless, I will bring health and healing to it; I will heal my people and will let them enjoy abundant peace and security. Jeremiah 33:6 (NIV)

I need to mention that everyone's healing journey is different. The first nail for me was forgiving myself and having to write a personal note to each of my children. I can't tell you the emotional days I endured during this period. It took me days to complete another step on my journey to forgiveness and healing.

I found comfort in just journaling my thoughts during this healing time. I suggest after this chapter before you move on to the top hurt on your cross just journal. I think it is important to get your thoughts out. What are you wrestling with; is it fear or anxiety? Maybe you know you are supposed to write to someone and send it, but this is just too risky for you right now. I would advise you to stay in prayer.

I spent these days reading the Bible and Oswald Chambers' Daily Devotional; there is a daily devotional for each day of the year. I find the message to be timely regarding what I am to focus on for the day.

Once I gained the courage to proceed up the cross of hurts, I found it very freeing with each letter I wrote. As I wrote each letter as I moved up the cross, I was not prompted to send the letter but to burn them. This is always going to be a question in your mind, whether to send, or burn the letter. God may even prompt you to confront the person. However, God does not call us to put our lives in danger when we proceed up the nails of hurt. For instance, if you were abused by someone, God will probably not ask you to confront this person, unless, of course, it is for court purposes.

With each letter I wrote I expressed all the feelings I experienced with the incident that happened. It was as though I was in front of the person, just pouring out the hurt they had caused me in my life. It was so freeing. I immediately felt a sense of peace and closure.

The Letters

Years ago when I was married I remember spending hours at counseling, about a situation that happened to me at Frosh Week during my first year at University. I want you to picture the situation and how shameful one would feel. I came from a very protective Catholic home and ventured out to new territories with which I had no prior experience. My sister and I were known for being green, and we were well respected in our teenage group of peers.

I remember my first week of University, Frosh week, one of the first nights our female house was invited to another male residence for activities and pub night. I went with a group of other girls and we had way too much to drink. I was not used to this newfound freedom and stayed on way later than I should have. I remember this handsome senior male eyeing me and he sat down and bought me a few drinks. We had chatted about lots of things throughout the evening, but I do remember sharing with him that I was a virgin and had planned to be until I married the right person. The only other thing I remember is being in his room, and being taken advantage of, a frosh girl who was intoxicated. The next day I was ready to quit university. I remember crying at my sisters' apartment and my parents coming to visit; I couldn't tell them what happened but I just kept begging them to take me home.

This one incident that occurred to me had a huge impact on my subsequent marriage. I was advised to be set free from this person by forgiving myself for the shame I felt, but also I had to forgive him for what he took away from me. It was twenty years later and I got the courage to call this person and say that I forgave them. I remember the conversation; I said if I had bumped into him years before, I would have run the other way. I knew during that time I had bitterness and an unforgiving heart. I went on to tell him that only through the grace of God and becoming a Christian, that I forgive him for taking away what was so precious to me, my virginity. I went on to say God forgave him too. He replied that it was just what guys did back then. I said "Well it isn't what God intends for guys to do to females; true gentlemen would never have done such a thing and you need to ask for forgiveness to be set free. I am free as I have been obedient for my part in extending forgiveness to you." The conversation ended.

There will be times when you are on your forgiveness journey and you are prompted like I was to either send the letter or call. The responses you receive will not always be what you hoped for, but the main reason for the letter or call is you have confronted and have been obedient to what God is calling you to do. You don't have any idea down the road how that one conversation or letter will have an impact on the person that hurt you.

God is in the business of changing lives and we need to trust Him that there was a purpose even if at the time there didn't appear to be. You must understand that the steps to forgiveness are for your healing and freedom from being bound to another person. You will receive freedom but even though forgiveness is offered to another it doesn't always mean they will respond and ask for your forgiveness for the hurt they did to you.

As I mentioned earlier it took me weeks after dealing with the first hurt to move my way up the cross of hurts. I remember the day I started to move up the cross and I wrote four letters to four different people with regards to four different hurts. In one day I poured my heart out of how each of those four events had impacted my life. I think my first nail drained so much out of me that I felt I just wanted to get through these other hurts all at once. I couldn't imagine having to feel such an emotional drain with every nail. I have to say, writing the letters, expressing my emotion, and shedding tears, all became much easier as I made my way up the cross. That top nail on the cross was staring me right in the face and I was avoiding it at every cost.

You will proceed up the cross of hurts in your way as God leads you. The cross of hurts is a very personal journey. The reason I had my private prayer room and my husband had his room was to allow our own private prayer time with God. Neither of us needs to see the other's cross of hurts unless God calls us to share or we feel a need to do so. This is a personal journey, but I have to say the fact both of us completed this journey together has had immense healing on our relationship. I would suggest relationships that journey through this forgiveness and healing will be better able to understand their partners' journey if they too complete the journey together.

Let's pray:
Heavenly Father we come to You today with our cross of hurts and are ready to begin our healing process of writing letters to each person on our nail of hurts. As we look over the hurts and surrounding events help us to be real before You when writing letters to each person; release all the resentment, anger, bitterness, and shame that built walls around our hearts. Even though these people may not even realize the impact their actions or words had on us help us to find closure and healing in the process of forgiving them. We ask for healing in Jesus' name. Amen

Reflections and steps to complete
Step 4

1) Be vulnerable in writing a letter to each person on your cross. This will be done over many days or weeks. Let God lead you in this process.
2) Journal your thoughts as you tackle each person on your nail of hurts cross.

Step 5

1) Pray and ask God if you are to burn the letter, send the letter,

or confront the person who hurt you.

2) Were you wrestling with God? If yes what were you wrestling with God about?

3) Leave your last nail on the cross for Chapter 5 Truth.

Group discussion or personal reflection

You may want to share your answers within your bible study or small group.

After reading the bible verses in this chapter, which verse spoke to you the most when dealing with each hurt in terms of writing the letter and following through with God's leading with what to do with the letter, burn, send, or confront?

1) Why do you look at the speck of sawdust in your brother's eye and pay no attention to the plank in your own eye?"Mathew 7:3 (NIV)

2) Nevertheless, I will bring health and healing to it; I will heal my people and will let them enjoy abundant peace and security. Jeremiah 33:6 (NIV)

You have now completed the fourth and fifth steps in forgiving the hurts in your life. Be proud of yourself. Pray and ask God with whom He would like you to be vulnerable in sharing your steps to forgiveness.

The Letters

28

CHAPTER 4 HEALING

We demolish arguments and every pretension that sets itself up against the knowledge of God, and we take captive every thought to make it obedient to Christ. 2 Corinthians 10:5. (NIV)

Reflect on whether or not you felt a sense of healing or a release of anxiety or worry after writing your letters. If you are still feeling anxious, cry out to God about what he wants you to do next.

After writing a forgiveness letter to my dear children, I thought the anxious feelings would dissipate. They did for a time, but I was still feeling things were not resolved. God was calling me to rewrite the letters and send them each a separate letter. After I wrote the letters and sent them, it was instant peace. This was not until a week later, after I wrestled with God as to whether he wanted me to burn or send the letters. My prayer is that you are feeling a sense of peace and healing from completing steps 4 and 5.

I have to be honest that for months after my trauma I was experiencing a numb feeling and was absent from any kind of connection to God. I was upset and angry at God for allowing my situation to happen. But it didn't stop there, I was bitter and it showed. I remember calling a pastor and chatting to him about what happened and at first, he appeared so understanding with regards to the trauma. But later when meeting with him and my husband I sensed he was insinuating that forgiveness could be possible down the road and I looked at him as though he had two heads. Then to top things off he said you may not want to share this story in any sort of group setting as it may be too much for people to understand. So I was not even feeling supported by Christian people whom I thought would be a safe place to heal and come to terms with what I was going through. Todd and I felt very much alone, and I am sure my bitterness was apparent, but at the moment, that was where I was. I needed someone to meet me in this bitter state not jump the bitter state to forgiveness.

So I am going to tell you that if you have just gone through a traumatic event and you feel like you do not feel ready for the healing steps to forgiveness that is ok. Trust me I know what you are going through. I resented anyone even implying I was to forgive the person that harmed me. If you are a counselor, friend, or pastor reading this, I caution you about suggesting forgiveness to a victim who has been through a traumatic event. I would suggest you listen to the victim and allow them to wallow in their hurt, going through the phases of trauma they are facing one phase at a time.

I experienced the following four phases:
- The first phase for me was numbness or some may call it shock. During this phase I didn't feel I was even a part of the earth or my surroundings; I was trying to make sense of what happened.
- The second phase was bitterness and anger at the person, the event and anyone who did not believe the truth.
- The third phase was retribution; I wanted the person to be stopped and I wanted justice and truth to be known.

- The fourth phase was giving over to God the trauma and going through the forgiveness stages.

Insinuating the victim move on any other step before the trauma takes it natural course would be to downplay their hurt and trauma and would not allow the person to properly heal.

Trauma, like the death of a loved one, has different stages. Usually, when a person grieves the death of a loved one, the person is numb and may be in this state of numbness for months. If you have ever been around someone deep in pain there are no words to describe it; they just need someone to be there to show they are present and care. They don't want quick fixes or cures to their grieving process they just want to feel loved and heard.

If you have never experienced the death of a loved one or other traumatic event it would be very difficult for you to understand. The understanding comes from walking alongside someone who is in deep pain and you will get firsthand the stages. Numbness, bitterness and anger, sadness, and tears are just a few emotions. The person may want justice and to any extent will want to get this justice. All said and done, they are probably upset with God for allowing such a circumstance to transpire in their life.

The worst thing you can do is isolate yourself from them because you don't want to hear about the situation anymore. I get that, but just think for a minute about the person who needs someone, and that someone might be you. Pray if God is calling you to be there for them, because you may be their only lifeline.

I know, I know what you are saying, you feel at times like Richard Dreyfuss in the movie" What about Bob" and you are worn out from dealing with the same old conversation. I remember one of my friends saying Lise-Marie, you just have so much drama in your life. If I could switch places and have peace what do you think I would pick? A peaceful life or a chaotic life, I can guarantee you the latter for sure.

Allow the person to chat about God authentically. Don't tell the person that they should not be angry at God. That is not what they want to hear. Just listen to what they need. At this stage, they need to know you care and will be there throughout the process: a kind gesture, a hug, and reassurance that everything will be ok.

I was a little distant from God because of this traumatic event. So what does one usually do when they have closed off God and need healing? I decided I was going to control my destiny because I trusted God and I was let down. I believed I was going to bring this person to own their actions if it was the last thing I do. I believed this person needed to pay for the hurt they caused me and others in the past year and a half. With everything we did the event just kept surfacing and the bitterness became more and more. I was drained and I decided I would have to find another way to heal.

I had mentioned earlier during COVID I had managed to start a walking group in my neighborhood, so this helped a great deal in giving me a somewhat normal existence. I could chat about surface events and laugh about silly things. In time, that became not enough.

I decided to masquerade the pain by starting a new project. This was a perfect remedy to not fixate on what was happening in my life. I bought an old 2005 travel trailer cheap and I decided to renovate it. In a sense, I looked at the trailer like the garbage that was happening in my life and I just wanted to make it look beautiful. Somehow, I had to try and get through this ugliness and survive. The trailer was the perfect project because, with every step I made in renovating the trailer, I could see progress, and the ugliness of the old trailer transformed into becoming new and more beautiful.

The walls and cupboards were dark brown and the floor was also old and dark. I sanded down every cupboard and painted the wood white. The brown that looked grubby was now brand new, white as snow. I placed nice black handles on the white cupboards that I bought off Amazon and it just made the doors pop. The walls were painted white. I threw out all the flooring and my husband and I put new flooring down. I would work on that trailer from the minute my husband left for work, until bedtime. I made new cushion covers and curtains. After months of prepping this old trailer, she sparkled when all said and done. We had my land in St. Martin's bush cut and gravel put in. Then after the trailer renovation, my husband and I built a beautiful deck. This second project got us through the fall months.

I recall our neighbors saying "My goodness you are spending so much time on that old trailer and at your land in St. Martins, we never see you anymore." But that old trailer like me needed some tender loving care. I felt so much pleasure in making the old trailer beautiful because it took my mind off the mess that surrounded my world. We could escape to the woods of St. Martin's and build a beautiful deck and all seemed just right. But was it? No!

God was laughing up in Heaven at Lise-Marie. "So you think you are going to be able to just shove down all the areas of your life by filling your schedule with things to do?" Then bang, my relationship with Todd started to take a whole new dimension. I could sense the walls of bitterness and anger surfacing in his life. I didn't feel connected to him, but both of us were dealing with the trauma situation differently.

Problems weren't new to us but now those problems were becoming more and more frequent and we started distancing ourselves. Our marriage was on the rocks and when I would ask him a question he would become defensive and angry. Once anger started I just shut down and the walls started to build. This was not what I thought would happen, as I was looking for a husband that would protect and love me with all I had been through and he so desperately wanted to but didn't know how; he wanted it all to go away. It is interesting how the devil was having a field day because I was not drawing close to God but trying to do things in my own strength.

I started writing this book and began to pray for healing, and God never gave up on me. He was waiting for me to exhaust every other avenue of healing. I then had to realize I needed to give my life over to God - again. After this revelation Todd and I started drawing closer to God. We found a new church to attend that was smaller and more personable. But all in all, we were not coming to terms with the major trauma event that occurred. Both of us suppressed the events, and how we were dealing with the unimaginable situation. We were each suffering our individual trauma surrounding the event and it was having a huge impact on our marriage. We were not feeling safe and trusting that we would stick together through these traumatic events.

After many quarrels that ended in his anger and resentment surfacing, I had enough of Todd's angry words, and he had enough of my mistrust. One day, we had a heated discussion surrounding many unresolved issues, and Todd said, "You don't have to worry because we are through." Those words hung on like a dagger in my heart. I truly thought it was over. We had major issues and it was usually me saying I had enough but this time it was him who said "That's it."

This blow up came the day before the police were coming to my house to interview me. I felt so hurt. Todd wasn't there when I needed him. This blowup started simmering two days prior, Todd was angry because of my failed attempts to get him to understand my needs. I knew there were areas of our lives that were not right because we were not connected in a deep and meaningful way. I would try to explain how I was feeling and how his distance made me feel so very much alone. He would respond with defense and tell me that things were not going to change if I didn't get over my trust issues.

Once again the healing journey took a different twist. No longer was I feeling the need to forgive a harmful action against me, now it was a matter of trying to save our marriage. I looked up counseling online as I knew that there was an aftermath to addiction in Todd's past that he used to numb the pain of an extreme trauma of losing a sibling to a gun accident, and as well as two failed marriages; now this traumatic event. These factors combined with my trust issues were taking a huge toll on our marriage.

Knowing we both came into this marriage with baggage we both apologized and forgave each other for our part in the upset. We agreed to begin our 30-day Forgiveness and Healing Journey together.

I did appreciate during this time having Christian people who rallied to pray for our marriage and healing from this event. Once we started spending time in our prayer room and completing the 30-Day Forgiveness and Healing Journal we saw a huge difference in our communication skills. He was being more attentive. I trusted more. Now are things perfect? No! But I will say we are focused on healing our wounds so we can be better together.

My online searching led me to a counselor I felt could help us. Unfortunately, he was all booked up. He knew we needed help and said he would try to get us in as soon as he could. In the meantime, he mentioned watching videos. Well, let me tell you those videos were life-changing. We started watching the videos and it was like my life was flashing before my eyes. I was living with a person who had intimacy issues; there was a name for this condition. If you have ever read about this condition it is emotionally draining. Your spouse is unable to connect in a deep and meaningful way; they avoid contact with regard to intimacy. (i.e., emotionally, physically, spiritually, and sometimes financially). I wondered why this was happening and truly don't know enough about the condition; however, I knew, as my husband watched the video with me, he realized it was him. We are now trying our utmost to face our marriage issues and get help. We are purchasing all videos and material on the issue so we can face it together.

So beware that setbacks will happen on your Forgiveness and Healing Journey; we are not only healing from the trauma of last year but also from an emotionally damaged relationship in need of repair. My prayer to you if you are going through a traumatic event and also finding it is tearing your marriage apart, that you seek help from a qualified counselor. I looked everywhere online to match a counselor for our specific issues.

Every relationship has baggage; the most important piece is accepting the part you play and healing from past traumas as they hinder your marriage from being all it can be. It is difficult to be salt and light to a hurting world when you are suffering.

Be aware that the devil will do his utmost in creating barriers in relationships especially when the two people are trying to pray, and trying to serve God. This is when a couple has to be more cognizant of when attacks are occurring and put on the armor of God and fight back the attacks of the devil. The Bible verse that comes to mind is,

Be self-controlled and alert. Your enemy the devil prowls around like a roaring lion looking for someone to devour. Resist him, standing firm in the faith, because you know that your brothers throughout the world are undergoing the same kind of

sufferings. And the God of all grace, who called you to his eternal glory in Christ, after you have suffered a little while, will himself restore you and make you strong, firm, and steadfast. To him be the power forever and ever. Amen. 1 Peter 5:8-11(NIV)

I am happy to say Todd and I went to a Family Life Retreat in St. Andrews, NB. We both knew we needed to build trust and oneness in our marriage. We both wanted to work towards creating a life pleasing to God. God was so timely that both Todd and I would contest that this marriage retreat was a lifeline that we desperately needed. The presenters were authentic about their marriage struggles some of which we can relate to. We left this weekend retreat feeling hopeful and ready to start a new chapter in our marriage. They provided us with tangible tools to build oneness in our marriage. Amen.

One of the things I would suggest if you are going through a trauma and finding it is affecting your marriage is to begin praying daily together to work towards healing. Don't allow bitterness and resentment to take a foothold. Practice the steps to forgiveness; communicate in a non-confrontational way. These steps to forgiveness will be mentioned in a later chapter. I found it helpful to deal with issues as they arise than letting them take a foothold and allowing walls to be built.

Another suggestion is to find ways to find joy and laughter in your life. We turn to Ken Davis and other Christian comedians that look at life through a different lens- the lens of laughter. The Bible states:- *"A cheerful heart is good medicine, but a crushed spirit dries up the bones." Proverbs 17:2.(NIV)* Laughter is so important to have in every relationship.

Last night Todd found a YouTube video for us to watch together called "Laugh Your Way to a Better Marriage" with Travis Bieberitz. I would recommend couples watch this because Travis gives excellent insight into the differences between men and women and why we have communication problems. But he does it in a very humorous way.

Todd and I didn't feel our life was so different than other married couples when we listened as the speakers addressed personal conflicts that arise in their marriage in a humorous but enlightening way.

We also found a common activity we could participate in, other than TV. We started playing pickleball on Tuesday and Thursday nights. This has had a wonderful impact on our marriage because we socialize with others, and enjoy a healthy sporting activity that isn't too taxing on the body. Pickleball is easy to learn, suitable for the midrange athlete as evidenced by the many middle-aged participants. I pray that you find a healthy activity that you can enjoy while you are on your Forgiveness and Healing journey.

Let's pray:
Heavenly Father we come to You today with our healing journey and are ready to begin our healing process. As we look over our life, relationships with our loved ones, help us to be real with our life. We ask you to protect us from any of the attacks from the enemy that are hindering our healing journey to forgiveness. Help us to put on Your armor of love to fight back when attacks occur. We want to have a heart of forgiveness towards our spouse and loved ones; release all the resentment, anger, and bitterness quickly, so we do not build walls around our hearts. Help us to respond in a loving way even when we feel we are being attacked. Forgive us for our shortcomings when we do not respond in a Christ-like way with our loved ones. We ask for healing in Jesus' name. Amen.

Reflections and steps to complete
Step 6
1) Reflect on whether or not you felt a sense of healing or a release of anxiety or worry after writing your letter. If you are still

feeling anxious cry out to God about what he wants you to do next.

2) Write down what you did next.

Group discussion or personal reflection
You may want to share your answers within your Bible study or small group.

After reading the Bible verses in this chapter, which verse spoke to you the most when dealing with healing and setbacks?

1) *We demolish arguments and every pretension that sets itself up against the knowledge of God, and we take captive every thought to make it obedient to Christ. 2 Corinthians 10:5.*

2) *Be self-controlled and alert. Your enemy the devil prowls around like a roaring lion looking for someone to devour. Resist him, standing firm in the faith, because you know that your brothers throughout the world are undergoing the same kind of sufferings. And the God of all grace, who called you to his eternal glory in Christ, after you have suffered a little while, will himself restore you and make you strong, firm, and steadfast. To him be the power forever and ever. Amen. 1 Peter 5:8-11(NIV)*

3) *A cheerful heart is good medicine, but a crushed spirit dries up the bones. Proverbs 17:2.*

You have now completed the sixth step in forgiving and healing the hurts in your life. Be proud of yourself. Pray and ask God whom He would like you to be vulnerable in sharing your steps to healing with.

Healing

CHAPTER 5 THE TRUTH

Then you will know the truth, and the truth will set you free. -- John 8:32(NIV)

Jesus answered, "I am the way and the truth and the life. No one comes to the Father except through me." –John 14:6(NIV)

The importance of speaking the truth as a Christian sets you apart from worldly people. The Bible is a guide to help Christians speak the truth in love. Speaking truth and accepting truth builds relationships, whereas speaking the truth and having people not believe your truth builds walls and creates division.

Many times, as Christians, we miss opportunities to speak the truth in the lives of our loved ones, so they too will understand what it means to be a Christian and walk with God. Recently, we gathered around our dinner table with the family, and the topic of death came up and how we do not want to be in pain. Many have suggested ways to lessen the pain of death and leave the earth sooner. As a parent and Christian, I gently tried to remind those at the table that Christians believe that God decides the timing of our death and that he too will decide when we leave the world.

Christian or not, it is a topic that needs to be addressed, as we live in a world where they are saying that you have a choice when you wish to die. If you have mental health problems you can decide to end your life. I realize there are always exceptions in every circumstance when a person is in severe pain and the length to which we decide to continue with medication to prolong a life, but it truly needs to be brought to prayer, so there is peace with God in the final decisions we make.

I had a dream last night that I believe God ignited, so I could clearly explain what I meant in the previous paragraphs. In the dream, I was walking in this high-rise city and birds flew around. I spotted an unusually large bird that looked like a parrot but was much larger. His head was enormous and there was even a tree stub growing from the side of his head. It was clear that this bird was aged. As I approached the bird, he appeared distressed. This old bird shared that he had been in this world and flown over this city when the settlers first inhabited the land. At that time there were fields but no buildings. People began to develop their lives. The air was clean. Now, he was old and tired of flying over the city with its pollution and high-rise buildings. The bird looked extremely sad and said, "I want to go home to my Father." I was about to approach the old bird on the ground and pray that our Heavenly Father would take him home.

My husband woke me up to kiss me before leaving for work and the dream was clear for me to share with you today. I think the message God was trying to convey in my dream was the words from the bird's mouth that he was ready to go home to His Father. As Christians in situations where our loved ones are suffering, our calling is to pray and ask God to help this person before us to be ready to go home to their Heavenly Father, and then pray that God releases them from their pain.

We need to be bold to speak of the truth in love and respect, or we are not being of any earthly good while on this earth. A gentle reminder is that it is God who controls the circumstances surrounding death, not man as much as a man would like to think he does. We cannot fully describe the depth of any situation over which God has control and what lives will be impacted in the process. I go back to the cross, and the pain Christ had on the cross. The pain we endure in our life could never measure the pain He had on the cross.

God gifted me at a very young age to always tell the truth. My mother would come and ask me something, and she knew I would not be able to tell a lie as it was written all over my face. As I grew in my Christian walk, the Holy Spirit would convict me about speaking full truths.

My recent encounter with speaking the truth about a harmful situation that happened to me and the overwhelming sadness I felt when others did not speak the truth and questioned the truth brought me to building walls of resentment. I needed to face this truth and forgive those who were involved either indirectly or directly surrounding the truth.

Due to privacy reasons and ongoing investigation, I am unable to speak about this incident. I want you to know that any incident of trauma, whether it is someone close to you dying or sexual abuse, has a lasting impact.

My husband and I were able to rally around one another through this incident as he at a very young age knew about trauma and the effect it has on a person. He went through years of pain and suppressed feelings and emotions around the death of his brother. He closed everyone out of his life and he went inward which later affected his relationships with others.

I am not sure where you are with your truth but I do know the importance of being around empathetic people who are loving and kind and are willing to listen to the pain you are feeling with regards to the trauma you had to face.

Even though we would assume we would receive empathy for the pain we are facing, it is interesting how you truly see the people in your life who respect you in times of need and who are there to support you. So, let us talk about that for a minute. What does a person need from anyone when they experience a traumatic event? First, they need you to listen; just listen to every tear shed, every angry word spoken, justified or not. I was blessed to have a few dear friends who were there for me during this phase. This is called the numb bitterness hurt pity stage. I didn't want to hear of any quick fixes or lists of dos and don'ts. I just wanted someone to hear me and comfort me during this phase. If you are reading this and have just gone through a traumatic event, find a safe place to talk to someone; even if it is a paid counselor because your family members do not believe your truth. Trust me it will be worth every penny you pay. If you are not able to afford a counselor there are nonprofit organizations online that will assist you by calling their 1-800 number or, you may feel more comfortable in asking your church for direction.

The first phase is the numb, bitter, hurt, and pity phase, and you may be in this bitter stage for months or even years, but allow yourself to have all the mixed emotions that this stage brings. At this stage, you may just want to be alone with God, crying and being real before Him. I remember crying out to him. Why? Why? Why?

I was comforted by the scripture reading, **In my anguish, I cried to the Lord and he answered by setting me free. The Lord is with me; I will not be afraid. -- Psalm 118:5-6(NIV).** Because not only were my husband and I dealing with the present trauma event, we were dealing with so many other issues in our marriage that this was like the last straw.

I truly did not know how I was going to deal with things and trust me I did not do a good job. Todd was quiet, reserved, and dealt with the truth and wanted to move on. I was shocked, but at the same time bitter and wanted justice. I was so determined the person was not going to hurt anyone else.

I took the role of the protector and detective all in one; I am sure God was up in Heaven laughing as I went around like a mad woman. He was probably thinking "Oh ye of little faith. I have this one. Trust me." I look back on this phase and I now can honestly say I needed to go through every emotion throughout this phase. Would I want to stay in this phase? No! I could not stay there long as I knew I was becoming a very bitter woman. I did not even like to be around me.

If you are in this phase right now I would suggest putting the book down and allowing the emotions you are feeling to surface. I mentioned in Chapter One that when hurting, you need to feel and go through the hurt. If you can relate to being that person who wants justice and you are bitter, trust me, it is a lonely place but you will get through it in your time. Surround yourself with the loving arms of friends and family and a trusted counselor. Cry out to God and be real before Him. He is waiting for you to turn to Him; you might not be ready to give it all over to Him right now because you are understandably in protective mode. I knew I was, and it felt good to take control of a life that was so out of control.

We started confiding in Christian people and appreciated the first meeting when sharing the truth. The only thing we found was that people were not equipped to deal with such a bizarre traumatic event. Both my husband and I needed support but each of us needed a different kind of support. I needed the support of being a victim and he required support for grieving.

We continued to go to Bible studies to stay connected and focus only on God and fellowship. It was like an escape from reality for us until the truth started festering and causing dissension in our marriage.

If you are the listening ear to a victim and you want to know what to do, we listed a few suggestions that we could have used as a couple during this traumatic event:

1) When the truth is revealed to you, just listen.
2) Think of this sharing as a gift from God. This person is being vulnerable in sharing with you.
3) Allow the person to get out all their emotions; tears, anger, hurt, shame and frustration.
4) Ask the person what they need most from you in the upcoming days, weeks, or months.
5) If the person says they are okay, this may be their defense mechanism, and they may still need support. I would suggest that you call them at a certain time each week.
6) Reassure them that your conversations are private.
7) Set aside one hour a week to be there for this person(s), check-in by phone.
8) Please never tell the victim that they should not share their truth. We had a member of a church caution us about speaking our truth to people in the church, as other members may find it too much.

With regard to number 8, I am not saying we were publicly speaking about what happened because it was private. What we needed was a safe place where people would surround us in love, who would meet and pray with us. Maybe even call to invite us for supper, but what we did not need was to feel any more alienated. We were very cautious about whom we told, but I am going to tell you now that victims need to share their stories whenever they feel God's prompting.

We found that the truth was not addressed at any level. We were hurting, and we now understand what it feels like to be a victim and have little or no support. It is almost like being re-victimized. If you are in this place, my heart goes out to you. It is a pretty lonely place to be. I would strongly suggest that you continue to share with a support group or seek Christian counseling.

We found that there was comfort in knowing the truth was prompted by our Heavenly Father when he revealed the truth without me mentioning it to both my friend and my husband. We then realized that we needed to rely on our Heavenly Father to see us through this traumatic event. What the enemy meant for evil, we had to believe that God would and could bring something good to the surface. It is God who decides the timing of this, and it is He who orchestrates the events surrounding the truth. I know this step, the truth step, is a very difficult one but, when you are ready, God will be there supporting you on this necessary step for your journey to forgiveness and healing.

When I prayed aloud with a Christian friend, immediately following my husband was told the truth from God. Todd told me that God revealed the truth to him the day my friend and I prayed aloud. I asked him at what time. My friend and I prayed between 9:00-9:30 a.m. and God revealed the truth to Todd during his work break at 10:00 a.m., many miles away.

This in itself was a miracle. I want you to think about that miracle for one minute. If God did not speak the truth to Todd, what might have been the outcome? Could anyone live with another if they do not walk beside them in truth? I know as a couple that we could not be around anyone, family or friends, who did not believe the truth after this event.

So, when you are there as a support to a loved one or friend the most important thing you can do is reassure them that you believe their truth and you stand by them in their truth; I cannot emphasize this enough.

Todd and I were very blessed to have family members and friends rallying together to support us.

Let's pray:
Heavenly Father we come to You today with the truth for You to use for Your Glory. As we look at the truth and surrounding events, help us see how Your hand was in every circumstance surrounding the truth. Even though people do not believe the truth, we know that You have a purpose and plan for this truth because You showed us the truth. Allow us to continue to be real before You, with all our emotions: anger, bitterness, shame, and resentment. We know You, and only You can release us from the hurt and bitterness we carry in our hearts. We ask for healing in Jesus' name. Amen

Reflections and steps to complete

Step 7: Be Vulnerable in writing out detail by detail the truth behind the hurt
1) Begin praying today for God to reveal which hurt(s) and the truth(s) surrounding the hurt(s) are priorities for you to deal with first. Your truth may never have been told before. You may feel shame or have not dealt with forgiving yourself for the part you played in the hurt. What is your biggest hurt? Who is God calling you to be vulnerable in sharing this hurt with?

2) Spend time in prayer asking God to bring to mind the truth behind the hurt.

3) Write down the "who, what, when, and where" of your truth.

Step 8: Placing the truth on paper
1) Using the information in step 7, write down your truth in a story form.

Group discussion or personal reflection

You may want to share your answers within your bible study or small group.

After reading the bible verses in this chapter, which verse spoke to you the most and did it assist you with your speaking truth?

1) *Then you will know the truth and the truth will set you free.--John 8:32(NIV)*

2) *Jesus answered," I am the way and the truth and the life. No one comes to the Father except through me." John 14:6(NIV)*

3) *"Every matter must be established by the testimony of two or three witnesses."*
 -- 2 Corinthians 13:1(NIV)

4) *In my anguish, I cried to the Lord and he answered by setting me free. The Lord is with me; I will not be afraid.--Psalm 118:5-6(NIV)*

You have now completed the seventh and eighth steps in speaking the truth about the hurt(s) in your life. Be proud of yourself. Pray and ask God with whom he would like you to be vulnerable in sharing your truth.

CHAPTER 6 BETRAYAL

Then one of the twelve—the one called Judas Iscariot--- went to the chief priests and said, "What are you willing to give me if I hand him over to you?" So they counted out for him thirty silver coins. From then on Judas watched for an opportunity to hand him over. --Matthew 26:14-16(NIV)

Imagine the pain Jesus must have felt when he was betrayed by one of his followers- when Judas turned Jesus in for thirty pieces of silver.

Have you ever felt betrayed before by someone you trusted: family, friend, or spouse? How difficult it is to have put the trust in someone, only to find out they have betrayed you by word or action?

I am so sorry if you, like me, began your journey by sharing your story and the truth only to have someone not believe your truth. The Bible asks us to go to the person who has offended us with two or more witnesses and share the truth. If they do not accept the truth, we are told to set them free.

I had a long-time friend of many years with whom I worked,

shared vacation weekends, and enjoyed many hikes. She would be classified, if you were to ask me eight years ago, as one of my dearest friends. We had been through so much as colleagues and as friends. I remember going on a weekend adventure with her sharing accommodations during the winter months. The cabin we were staying in had ice in front of it. We got all ready in our warm gear ready for our walking adventure when I slipped on the ice and ended up with a concussion. It kept us cabin bound for the weekend as I was not myself; I was a little dizzy. On the way out my friend told the establishment that we were looking for compensation as the ice should have been cleared and they agreed to give us a free night's stay.

Fast forward to the next trip we took together with a stay at the same establishment, and on our way there I said, "This trip will be paid for." She responded, "We will chat about it later." When we arrived I insisted that we didn't have to pay to the man at the front desk. He said something to the effect that they were not aware of this because they were new owners etc. My friend wasn't pressing the point, but I did. I got the establishment's number to call and she allowed me to go through the whole procedure only to find out that she had already used that free night with her sister earlier that year.

So the free night provided to us as compensation for my concussion, she decided to use with her sister. Not only did she lie to me, but she allowed me to continue to call the new owner when she knew the truth. I was so hurt because I couldn't understand how a friend could do that to another friend. I knew I had to forgive her and I did- but our relationship has never been the same.

The trust in our relationship was broken over something so

unnecessary and avoidable. A simple, "I'm sorry," so I could understand would have gone a long way. Instead, she kept silent causing me to waste time and energy. And once the truth of the matter was revealed she justified her actions by saying she thought I would understand; there was no sense of any kind of remorse for the lying, withholding the fact she used the credit for herself and her sister. The withholding/lying that occurred was even more hurtful than the act of using the credit. It is one thing to forgive someone who betrays you when they are truly sorry for the hurt they caused you. But how do you forgive someone who betrays you and justifies it? This one incident changed our friendship and we no longer spend time together. I think there is a correlation between heartfelt forgiveness and forgiveness that is extended because you are caught. The bible states:

"Like a madman shooting firebrands or deadly arrows is a man who deceives his neighbour and says, "I was only joking!" -- Proverbs 26:18-19(NIV)

There is a story I used to read to my elementary students called "Someone Sees You" from the "Children's book of Virtues" edited by William J Bennett; I would read this story to teach young ones about morally making the right decisions. It goes something like this:

A father was asking his daughter to keep watch while he took some wheat from a neighbours field nearby their house. He convinced himself that his neighbour would not miss a little wheat from his field and it would make a nice pile for himself. After it was dark he took his daughter with him to keep watch that no one would see him. Just as the father was about to get wheat the little girl said "Someone sees you." The father would race back only to find his daughter with no one around. He would get frustrated and would begin again only to have his daughter say," Father, someone sees you." The Father came back for the second time only to find once again his daughter and no one else in sight. After the fourth time, he returned to his daughter and said, "Daughter every time I am about to take wheat from the field you tell me someone is watching. Why do you keep saying someone sees me?" The little girl replied to her father, "Someone does see you Father. Someone sees you from above."

Isn't this true about each day in our own life? As we go through life thinking our behaviour, our hurtful actions, and our betrayals go unnoticed, we are mistaken. God is watching our every action, all our words, and how we handle and confront the truth.

My husband and I felt the importance of sharing the truth to those who might possibly be affected. We learned a valuable lesson; as much as you think you know someone, you don't know until the truth is revealed.

After my husband and I shared the truth about my situation, we naturally felt people would believe the truth, only to find out that many changed their stories. We now have a glimpse of how Jesus felt when Judas betrayed him. This betrayal extended to many because they did not want to come to terms with the truth.

So how does someone respond to betrayal? I can honestly say I didn't do well. After calling the people who we felt might be at risk, knowing God wanted us to, we knew people did not want to believe the truth, because they had already came to their own conclusion surrounding the incidents.

The Bible states this with regards to betrayal, -- **After he had said this, Jesus was troubled in spirit and testified, "I tell you the**

truth, one of you is going to betray me." John 13:21(NIV)

It was not as shocking for me to later find out that people betrayed us. God warned me through someone close to us that we would be betrayed. At times, God will use others to heed the warnings. The Bible states:

See to it that you do not refuse him who speaks. If they did not escape when they refused him who warned them on earth, how much less will we, if we turn away from him who warns us from heaven? --Hebrews 12:25(NIV)

Important that we listen and not refuse to take warning from others on earth. These warnings could be from God speaking to us that danger is ahead.

When you are going through your Forgiveness and Healing Journey, you may come to a point like I did that the main hurt on the cross is something very difficult to share. In our situation, we had to share so that others would not be harmed. After we shared the truth, we felt the pains of betrayal; more nails on the cross of hurts. We had prayed before sharing; this was a very important step. Whether you feel it or not, God will be with you even if the result of the truth ends up being betrayal. This is a testimony of what obedience and trust can look like.

We also felt betrayal from those who did not want to accept the truth. Therefore, betrayal was a direct result because they were willing to brush the event under the rug.

Another betrayal we endured came from a church we were attending. We shared our story and no one from the church checked in on us to see how we were making out after going through such a traumatic event. We concluded that they were just not equipped to deal with such a trauma. Still, we wondered why they never called us to see how we were doing, especially when we had reached out for their help. This help could have been checking in once every two weeks, or advising us of a qualified counseling service that would be equipped to help us.

On top of that we had the disappointment of dealing with the police detachment. We were waiting each week for a follow up only to be given the run around. Once again, no one was equipped to handle this situation. Throughout our ordeal, my husband and I realized that with all the betrayal that occurred, we had to start enforcing personal boundaries.

I recommend that you too set healthy boundaries concerning the people who betrayed you after sharing the truth. My husband and I realized that the only way for us being truly at peace was to set boundaries.

I know personally, it was easy for me to set boundaries because I knew God was not calling me to put myself in danger. My calling was to forgive and I knew I could do this at a distance. Once my husband placed boundaries, our marriage started healing; there was a sense of peace that we knew the truth and it didn't matter what others thought. Our prayer was that God would eventually reveal the truth.

Other boundaries that come to mind involve relationships where someone has time, and time again, hurt you, and asks for forgiveness, only to continue hurting you in the same way. It is important for you to set healthy boundaries for your well-being. This will let the other person know you are serious about their actions and that their actions need to stop. For example, if a husband gets verbally abusive, you place a boundary that you leave the house when the ranting begins. God does not call us to be a doormat to abusive or hurtful behaviour. Continue to pray while asking God to guide you in making your boundaries in each of your betrayals. Seek counseling to have a clear path for setting boundaries.

With regards to the church we were attending, we decided we had to begin looking for a new church. If you are not being fed in the church you are attending, pray for God to lead you to a new church; one where you are connected to God and grow in the body of Christ with like minded believers. Currently we are attending a new church to see if we can be used within their church community. We are looking for an authentic church where we can plant our roots and begin to get involved as a married couple. But the key word is authenticity. It is so important that we live a life worthy of speaking truth and following God's direction with every step we take.

Let's pray:
Heavenly Father we come to You today with the betrayal we have felt from truth we have spoken. As we look upon the truth we pray that the truth is revealed to all so that we have a sense of peace with the truth you have brought forth. We ask you to look at the people who have betrayed us, (name each person) and release all the resentment, anger, and bitterness that we feel towards (name each person). Even though these people may not even realize the impact their actions or words have had on us, help us to find closure and healing in the process of forgiving. We ask for healing in Jesus' name. Amen

Reflections and steps to complete
Step 9
1) You have spoken truth and there are people who do not believe you and you have felt betrayed. Pray and ask God to reveal what boundaries are to be put into place in order for you to

feel safe. What is God calling you to do about boundaries and the truth?

2) Write down your boundaries and next steps. It would be helpful to share with someone how you feel about setting betrayal boundaries.

Group discussion or personal reflection

You may want to share your answers within your bible study or small group.

After reading the bible verses in this chapter, which verse spoke to you the most when dealing with the betrayal you encountered when speaking truth?

1) *Then one of the twelve—the one called Judas Iscariot--- went to the chief priests and said, "What are you willing to give me if I hand him over to you?" So they counted out for him thirty silver coins. From then on Judas watched for an opportunity to hand him over. --Matthew 26:14-16(NIV)*

2) *After he had said this, Jesus was troubled in spirit and testified, " I tell you the truth, one of you is going to betray me."--John 13:21(NIV)*

3) *See to it that you do not refuse him who speaks. If they did not escape when they refused him who warned them on earth, how much less will we, if we turn away from him who warns us from heaven? --Hebrews 12:25(NIV)*

You have now completed the ninth step in setting boundaries around sharing your truth and subsequent betrayals you encountered with speaking truth and betrayal in your life. Be proud of yourself. Pray and ask God whom He would like you to be vulnerable with in sharing your boundary step.

CHAPTER 7 GO! FEAR NOT

Have I not commanded you? Be strong and courageous. Do not be terrified; do not be discouraged, for the Lord your God will be with you wherever you go." --Joshua 1:9(NIV)

Through much heartache, I recall God calling me to step out in faith. In 2004 after my mother's death and my recent divorce, I felt change was necessary for my life. I typed in the computer job opportunities for teachers; much to my surprise up on the computer screen the words "exchange to Australia" appeared. I remember being down in the basement and yelling to my children who were upstairs "What would you think of going on a teacher exchange to Australia for a year?" A teacher exchange is an opportunity for two teachers from two countries to switch jobs for a time, sometimes for half a year, but most opt for a year's exchange. The three responded with "Really, could we?" I said, "We need to pray about this. We have to be sure all of us are on board; if one of us doesn't want to go it means we all don't go." They agreed.

I knew if God wanted us to go to Australia everything would work smoothly. The only roadblock I could see existing was their father not agreeing to our request. God is good! He saw the excitement in his children's eyes and agreed to allow them to go. Even though my extended family was on board, I felt I still needed a definite sign from God that this was His plan. I remember sitting in church and the minister saying, "Today I would like to say a prayer for the people in Australia." My children looked at me and said, "Is that sign enough?"

As we flew across the country miles from our home, tears streamed down my youngest daughter's face, and I couldn't console her by telling her it was going to be wonderful at the other end because I truly didn't know what we were facing. However, I knew without a doubt God had his hand in this adventure we were about to embark upon.

When we arrived at the airport it was extremely humid. My Exchange Partner's parents and relatives picked us up and we drove 300 miles from Adelaide into the wilderness. I could see the fear in my children's eyes as tumbleweeds were crossing our path and the city lights of Adelaide grew dimmer and dimmer. We finally reached our destination - a small rural place called Renmark with a population of approximately 7000. We were going to be living in an adjacent area known as Paringa. It had a population of about 500.

My main concern was being sure my children were involved in a church that had a strong youth group. I remember being very impressed that one lady from a Baptist church encouraged us to attend the Lutheran church down the street as it had a vibrant youth group. When I went in, I was greeted by the secretary who knew where I lived in New Brunswick because her husband studied as an engineer in Fredericton NB. The miles that separated my homeland from this faraway land just became closer. On top of that, she knew where I lived and her church was also having their youth group study "The Purpose Driven Life" by Rick Warren; I had just completed this book study. I remember thinking, "God is so good!" We planted our feet at that church and enjoyed many a potluck and fellowship with like-minded believers.

My faith grew so strong over the year, and I could see how God was using this event to build me up in my walk. During our first few days, we attended many events in our community and one was welcoming people who were becoming Australian citizens. There was a barbecue in the community, and I remember a man from South Africa speaking. He spoke with a strong faith in the Lord. Later his wife and I became good friends. She too was a teacher and she introduced me to "prayer walking" in the community. This was the first time I felt at ease with praying aloud outside. She taught me to begin by praising God and thanking Him ahead of time for all His blessings. I learned a great deal about praying with boldness, honesty, and thanksgiving. It was amazing how God worked in the lives of those around me when we prayed for them. The year flew by, and we were supposed to be spending Christmas in Australia, but we all agreed Christmas would just not be the same without family and snow, so we changed our flight and were able to fly into Moncton on December 24th at 11:00 pm.

I will never forget the beautiful greeting we received at the airport on Christmas Eve night after being away for a year. Every one of our family members were there to greet us. I walked into our home to find a Christmas tree lit up, garland streaming down our stair rail landing, presents under our tree, and a fridge filled with food. It was truly something out of a hallmark movie and my sister was at the forefront of it all. Loved, loved, loved is the only way we can describe the feelings we experienced that day; we truly felt that our presence had been missed. We had so many stories to share and my children had grown so much over the year we were away.

Every time God calls us out into the unknown, we rely on His presence in our life to sustain us through the adventure. As I mentioned earlier, I felt His presence throughout my journey in

Australia; His hand was in every facet of this trip and I could feel Him walking beside me as a teacher, Christian friend, and within my fellowship at Bible studies. I watched my children grow and experience a world different from home, but I also learned a valuable lesson about listening, truly listening to God, and trusting Him even if it didn't make sense.

Another time I felt a "Fear Not" and "Go" response was on a missionary trip to Trinidad in 2005. My children spent the week after Christmas with their father and this was always a time in my life where I felt a void so I prayed, and I found a missionary trip opportunity in Trinidad; I boarded a plane and set out to see where God would lead me. I stayed with a woman who was a Pentecostal minister, and her husband. We went to various orphanages in the area and learned first-hand the power of prayer and the gift of healing hands that our Father provides as a blessing through us to others.

I was brought up with a very praying mother who knelt before her Father every night before she went to bed. She would be someone I would name a prayer warrior. Many people asked my mother to pray for them and she earnestly did. I too felt God gifted me with prayer but also with the power of healing hands. I learned from this missionary trip to lay hands on the sick and watch God work a miracle on others through faith, prayer, and His will. Often when my children were young, I would lay my hands on the area they were feeling sick and ask God to heal their illness. I always felt God's presence in healing my children when they were ill. Another time I prayed over my mother and asked God to heal her when she was sick with cancer, and the doctors felt she had maybe weeks left. My brother flew home thinking her time was near. But God was gracious enough to hear my plea; we were blessed by our Heavenly Father to have her around for another year.

Usually when God asks us to Go, there is no holding us back.

There is without a doubt a knowing that you are being called to speak or move- now not later. Sometimes these events are received well and unfortunately, sometimes they are not.

I remember one time a dear relative was heading out on one of her many traveling adventures and the Lord prompted me to go to her. It was very early in the morning, and I remember thinking, are you sure God? But it was like a magnetic force, and I was not going to argue with God. So, I went to her door at about 6:00 am, gave her a big hug, and told her God asked me to talk to her. Through my tears I told her I just needed to affirm her faith and that she believed in the Lord. She reassured me she did have faith.

Later I remember her mentioning the event to me and her concern that I may be experiencing unnecessary anxiety. I smiled and then realized God still had work to do in her life. Sometimes as Christians, we need to do His will and then let go and this was one of those times. We can believe and share our beliefs but when our relatives or family or even our children become young adults they now have a choice to make outside the confines of the home they were raised in. We need to just continue to faithfully pray and TRUST God in His plan for our life and their life.

When God asks us to "Fear Not" and "Go" He is asking us to do the task solo. He has a blessing to give to us or wants to use us to be a blessing to others. Usually, there is a blessing that we receive that changes us. Years later in 2019, I came home from a Woman's Conference in New York and it was by far one of the most powerful events I have been to. I remember sitting in my living room feeling like my faith had been shaken from events that took place throughout the year and that I needed a powerful dose of the Lord's blessing. As Christians, we have to be careful not to grow too stagnate and complacent with the world around us especially if we are drowning and not fulfilling His plan for our life. Be careful and always stay in prayer. He has a perfect plan for you to accomplish but not stepping out will cause us to be fearful.

Sometimes we can be complacent in our lives and this is the time God may pull at our heart strings. I remember one particular weekend my husband happened to be busy with a target shooting event, so I figured it was an opportunity to find a women's retreat. I googled thinking something might possibly pop up in the area in which I lived, or at least in Canada, but no, God had another plan. I found a conference, but it was being held in New York. This was Tuesday and the conference was Friday. So, I said to my husband that if everything went smoothly and my Air Miles could cover the cost of a flight, I would be flying out this coming Friday for the weekend to a woman's conference. Fortunately, I have been blessed with a Christian man who encourages me to listen to God and so I had his blessing to attend.

Wow! What a blessing I received by not caving into fear. There was a voice in my head questioning me, saying, "You are doing this alone. Are you sure you want to venture out to the unknown?" What if I was tempted to succumb to the voice of doubt? We all have times we listen to that voice that we are not good enough, skilled enough, etc. Believe it or not, as we age, fear can cripple us and cause us to freeze in our present state when God is calling us to step into unknown territory, so we will grow in our walk and TRUST in Him. Each time I've stepped out and acted when I felt God's calling, I have been rewarded with blessings.

At this particular conference the Pastor told me twice, "You will touch millions of lives." I tried to look around the room to be sure she wasn't speaking to someone else. I felt a strong overwhelming sense of responsibility to our Lord to Fear Not and begin to step out and write this book. But I can honestly say if I had not stepped out and gone to this conference I wouldn't have been encouraged to begin writing again. He was preparing me for what I had yet to face- a fear came three years later that I would not ever have imagine would enter my life. But in that moment in time, He freed me from fear of the unknown and I stepped out to join a conference alone and He faithfully gave me the courage to step out. I thank Him daily for His faithfulness to me and not giving up when I had.

Thank you, Lord!

Nine years ago, a young man in his late teens became entrenched in worldly activities, becoming fixated on guns and developing little respect for authorities. He was getting involved in the wrong influences where Satan grasped hold of his life. He went from what the church and people in the neighbourhood described as a kind and quiet boy to someone they did not know. The parents were distraught as they tried to understand the path their son was going down; they home-schooled him in a Christian home. His parents had to ask him to leave the home.

On the night of June 4th, 2014, he shook our community as He went out on a shooting rampage killing police officers and sending fear into the community. I remember that event well because the full community was in lockdown and I was on my own. I felt the paralyzing grip that the enemy can have on lives as I locked the doors and stayed awake for fear he was going to enter my home. This went on for days and I never left the confines of my home.

I didn't realize the effect this event had on me until years later, when two young gunmen killed innocent bystanders in British Columbia and now Manitoba. The headlines read that they could be heading east so be on the alert. This news brought up the tragedy of my community's past, and I panicked unbelievably once again. This time even though my husband reassured me that it was far from us I still found myself locking all my doors and checking the news to see where they were spotted last. It was becoming an obsession because fear had a hold on me.

I stayed in my house on the days my husband was at work. But this is a way the enemy can control us and paralyze our life if we are not careful. God calls us not to live in fear but be bold in our endeavours. He will protect us, and we have to TRUST that whatever the circumstances or outcomes, His will, will be done. I can now see how FEAR is so crippling and if we are not aware of it; it can cause us to be out of God's will for our life.

I know right now that some of you may be questioning where was God protecting me when I was being abused? When my son or daughter was killed in a car accident? Those are legitimate questions that can only be answered, I believe, when you meet your Heavenly Father in Heaven and ask Him. I do believe we are safe in His arms, but that does not always mean we will be physically safe in this world. The stronger our connection with God the more peace we can have in the face of adversity. We may not understand the afflictions that happen all around us but we need to Trust God and not fear in the face of adversity. We all have times that we have had to face our fears.

I can honestly say I have never felt fear like the fear that entered my life since someone tried to harm me. I was so distraught that someone would want to do me such grave harm, I went into fear mode. This fear took over my life- day after day- week after week- month after month. During this time, I did not want to leave the confines of my home. I would draw the curtains, lock the door, and even lock my bedroom door. Have you ever been in that kind of overwhelming fear mode? Maybe through COVID, you were fearful of catching COVID, or transmitting COVID, or maybe you are in an abusive relationship where someone tried to harm you or is harming you?

This fear is like no other and unless you too have had a fear like that it is very hard to describe to another. I would call it crippling. Unlike the crippling effect that outside situations have on your life as described earlier in this chapter, this is the crippling effect of being harmed. I want you to know I understand what you are going through, and it may take you months, even years to get the courage to step out. Fear from even less traumatic events can be crippling.

How do you deal with the crippling effects of fear that takes over your life? All I can say is, it takes a great deal of time or at least it did for me. Eventually, I found comfort in knowing there were people in the neighbourhood who were walking each day and I could join them to feel somewhat normal. So just be easy on yourself. I read through the beginning of this chapter and looking back I wish I could go back to the freedom I felt with knowing God was walking right beside me. During this event, I knew God was beside me, it was just harder for me to grasp why He allowed this to happen to me.

I was definitely in a victim mentality, and I couldn't shake it. I was hurt, I was angry, I wanted justice and revenge. All the things that a victim feels, I felt. You name the emotion- I felt it. Was it right? It felt right for me at the time and for anyone to say, "Well, Lise-Marie you know a Christian shouldn't respond in that way." I would say," Walk in my shoes and then we will sit down and chat."

I felt secure in this state because I was controlling things. But guess what, I probably knew deep down I couldn't stay in this state forever. And neither will you, but at the time this is where I needed to be and you are where you need to be. Why? So, I could relate to you. Imagine if I just turned the other cheek like some Christians would tell you to do. Well then, we wouldn't have had much in common, would we? You would probably say, what's wrong with me that I can't snap out of it as she did? Brother or sister, there is no easy way through life's trauma, and I am not going to pretend there is because I would be lying to you, and I am not a liar. Did I get angry and frustrated? You bet! Did I cry and blame and want people to console me day in and day out? Yes! I wasn't the most pleasant person to be around, and watch out if you dared to challenge me during this time - I would shut you right out of my life.

Sound familiar? I wanted to be heard- not told what to do. It wasn't pretty and I am not going to pretend it was. I wasn't any earthly good in this bitter, victim state; yet God was waiting. He was patiently waiting for me to give over and trust in Him. God reminds us in scripture that He has plans for us, ***"For I know the plans I have for you, declares the Lord, plans to prosper you and not to harm you, plans to give you hope and a future."--Jeremiah 29:11(NIV).*** In His time, not mine He would somehow turn this terrible event into good. I just needed to somehow understand He was there even if I couldn't feel His presence because the pain was too great. These thoughts came to mind when I started allowing God to take control:

> **"We try to control our lives when our lives are out of control. We try to control our fears by trying to control our surroundings and loved ones. God calls us to "Fear not for I know the plans I have for you." We want human beings to fill a void only God himself can fill.**
> **Why?**
> **We see them in human form; they can speak to us in human form and acknowledge us in human speech. But then the human fails us, we must then acknowledge before God that we have failed to place Him first above all else.**
> **Then,**
> **We become humble before God and go to him in prayer. God does not want us to give human beings control. He wants us to Trust only in Him to control our everyday life. When we make prayer a part of our everyday life we see how God works where no human being could work. He changes lives. He has changed my life. He will change yours."**

Will you walk with me on the rest of this journey to Trust and see how God works and watch your life change when you give God full reign of your life?

Let's pray:
Heavenly Father we come to You today with all our fears and are ready to begin our healing process giving our fears over to You. As we look over our lives we see how Your hand has been a part of every intricate detail of our life. Help us to Trust in You to release all the fears we have kept and tried to control in our own strength. We see the impact of fear on our life and the lives around us. We give all our fears over to you so the enemy does not get a foothold on our life. We want to live free from fear so we can be used by You. We ask for healing of fear in Jesus' name. Amen

Reflections and steps to complete

Step 10

1) Reflect on a time you stepped out in faith. Did fear try to persuade you not to? What valuable life lesson did you learn by stepping out?
2) Has God been calling you to step out? Fear not? Discuss your fears with your small group. What is holding you back from going out?
3) Or maybe there was a crippling fear that took over your life- As a result of a Traumatic event? Remember to pamper yourself and do all that is needed to feel safe. Draw the curtains, and curl up under the sheets. Do what you need to do to feel safe. Scream out to God and ask the hard questions.

Group discussion or personal reflection
You may want to share your answers within your Bible study or small group.

After reading the bible verses in this chapter, which verse spoke to you the most when dealing with your fears?

1) Have I not commanded you? Be strong and courageous. Do not be terrified; do not be discouraged, for the Lord your God will be with you wherever you go."–Joshua 1:9(NIV)

2) "For I know the plans I have for you, declares the Lord, plans to prosper you and not to harm you, plans to give you hope and a future."-- Jeremiah 29:11(NIV)

You have now faced the fears in your life. Be proud of yourself. Pray and ask God whom He would like you to be vulnerable in sharing your fears.

CHAPTER 8 EXERCISE AND SOCIALIZE

Do you not know that your body is a temple of the Holy Spirit, who is in you, whom you have received from God? You are not your own; you were bought at a price. Therefore honor God with your body.--1 Corinthians 6:19-20(NIV)

Therefore encourage one another and build each other up, just as in fact you are doing. --1 Thessalonians 5:11(NIV)

I mentioned briefly in an earlier chapter that I started a walking group during COVID; this group was formed pre-trauma. Each morning a group of ladies in the neighbourhood would meet and go for a walk. It was a healthy way to get out and socialize during those COVID months of isolation. It was our mental well-being exercise. After the trauma event, I continued walking.

There was a time in my life, in my 30s and 40s, that I could not go a day without going to the gym, doing weights, swimming, or running. At that time I was much younger and I had a goal. I wanted to complete an Olympic triathlon which consists of a 1.5km swim, 40 km bike, and 10 km run- all in succession. To complete this triathlon, I had to be extremely dedicated to training in all three areas; swimming was the most difficult part of the race. I had completed sprint triathlons, roughly half the distance of an Olympic triathlon, but I wanted to say I fully completed a full Olympic triathlon before I hung up my gear.

I was told I had a fusion in my neck that was causing extreme migraines every time I swam in the pool. At first, I thought it was the chlorine from the water, so the doctor decided to send me to a neurosurgeon; he took x-rays of my neck only to find out my C2 and C3 vertebrae neck bones were fused at birth. I don't have the mobility most people have and he cautioned me about training and competing in triathlons because the continuous repetition of tilting my neck during freestyle stroke could damage my neck further. He went on to say if I ever received an extreme blow to the head possibly from a bike accident, it could leave me paralyzed.

All this information was a little more than I could handle as I did not want to be told I couldn't participate, but then the thought of being paralyzed wasn't something I wanted either. He agreed that I could continue to train and finish this one event that I was so focused on completing.

I remember the day of the event well; I drove to Nova Scotia with my daughter. We went to the race facilities the day before to get a lay of the land. I felt ready because I had trained so hard for the past few years. The following day was a beautiful and sunny day with warm temperatures. I started the race swimming in the lake but met with some opposition, there were large reeds I kept getting tangled up in. I almost gave up because it was difficult to have a smooth swim stroke. I managed to free myself from the weeds beneath me as I focused on finishing the swimming race. I got out of the water with wobbly legs after swimming 1.5 km and hopped onto my bike to complete the 40 km road race. This was the best part. I trained long and hard to get my legs strong enough for the hills I would face. If you are not familiar with triathlon events, sometimes they will hold the Sprint Triathlon Race, which is half the distance of the Olympic Triathlon Race at the same time. They have people who guide you through the race to indicate where to turn for the Sprint or Olympic race.

During the bike I got up to where I thought was the turn for the Olympic Triathlon turn. There were no flags indicating otherwise, so I proceeded to turn and head back to the start. I got off the bike and started to run my last stretch of 10 km. I got to the finish line and I was so happy to see my daughter. Unfortunately, I was met by one of the officials who said there was a bit of a discrepancy with my time. Something doesn't appear to be right. He went on to say I turned at the 10 km mark not the 20 km mark for the Olympics. I couldn't believe my ears, I truly thought they were joking but they weren't. I was devastated as I knew this would be the one and only Olympic Triathlon I would compete in.

With my head held low, I moped for the majority of the drive. Then we stopped at a gas station to get gas and a few goodies. When I walked towards the gas station door, I saw a man in a wheelchair. A little voice whispered in my ear, "That man wishes he could just walk 10 feet and you are complaining you weren't able to complete an Olympic Triathlon Race?" I quickly gave my head a shake, picked my chin up off the ground, and thought I am lucky, I can walk and I have nothing to feel downtrodden about.

We all have bodies that God gives us freely to look after. I don't believe my body defines who I am but I do believe if we take care of our body, like we take care of our heart, mind, and spirit we are doing what God asks us. As we age we don't have the same stamina as a younger person but we still have an older body to take care of. Anything we do in life should be measured through the lens of God. If we become too obsessed with exercising and our health, placing this above God or our spouse, this can be detrimental to our relationships. Everything should be done in moderation; a healthy balance of exercise, eating well, and spending time with God in prayer and with our spouse is important. Let's talk about some healthy ways we can take care of our bodies and our mental well-being.

During COVID people were isolated from community activity. As much as it was important to isolate for health reasons, it was difficult for many people to be away from family and friends for such a lengthy period. During COVID everyone had to learn to cope with change, juggling family and work; no longer being able to go to the gym or attend social activities.

Teenagers isolated in their homes suffered from lack of socialization with peers which took a toll on their mental health; the same way elderly people in home facilities struggled not receiving stimulation from the daily or weekly visits from family and friends.

In both situations, they relied solely on their establishments to provide socialization which became somewhat taxing on parents and homecare workers. I truly believe it was easier for the introvert to isolate during COVID as opposed to the extrovert. Introverts need time alone to rewire or boost their energy, whereas an extrovert needs socializing to give them the energy to move on.

I am an introvert, so the COVID isolation didn't affect me as much, except for the fact I wasn't able to see my family and grandchildren. Even after COVID and restrictions were lifted I continued to use COVID as an excuse to stay isolated, trying to deal with the fact someone tried to do grave harm to me. After months of being indoors, I realized I needed to get out and move.

Even though I am an introvert, I realized I was still in need of daily conversation, so I started walking with one of the ladies in my neighbourhood, being sure to wear our COVID masks. I live in a neighbourhood that consists of approximately fifteen houses within a round circular block. Everyone's property is approximately an acre and a half. We are not on top of each other, but you do get to know your neighbour- if you have any sort of interpersonal skills. I mentioned to this lady during one of our walks that we should start including other people on our circular road; low and behold before long we had ten women in our WhatsApp group.

Each morning, a post would be put on, and each morning, we would meet for our hour walk. It was a wonderful way to get through the COVID Phase and an excellent part of my healing through the trauma I was facing.

As I mentioned before, exercise is good at any age because it is healthy for your body, but we were also building a community by socializing at the same time. This form of exercise and chatting with others helped me a great deal in healing from the trauma because I could escape from my bitter state and find humor in our chats and conversations.

My husband and I started walking when he arrived home from work, so I was getting a double dose of exercise, and it felt wonderful. During the summer months, one of the ladies offered to show the rest of the group how to play pickleball. I would go a few mornings a week, and then Todd was given a lesson, and we started enjoying a few games with our neighbours.

In the winter months, we decided to start pickleball again. This time, we got more serious; we purchased racquets and joined the Shediac Pickleball League. We had so much fun. They welcomed us to their group and we continue to enjoy Tuesday and Thursday night pickleball activities.

Recently, a more experienced pickleball player has offered to assist me in learning new skills to improve my game. I was so encouraged by her step-by-step approach of having me play alongside her as a partner and receiving tips from an expert. She mentioned that some people decline her offer of help - not me! I was excited to learn more about the game and to progress. That's the wonderful thing about pickleball, you can choose to enjoy the game but not have the competitive nature common to more advanced players. This is a game for everyone.

I cannot emphasize the importance of exercising your body, so you have energy as you age. And like walking and talking benefit us physically and socially, pickleball has the same effect. Now that we are regularly going to pickleball, it has even helped our marriage become more enjoyable. Pickleball gets you socializing with others, and there is an opportunity to meet other people and possibly make friendships that otherwise would not be established.

During COVID there were many couples whose marriages ended in divorce because they were faced with dealing with their spouse day-in and day-out. This can take a toll on a marriage. It is important to have an equal balance between being together with others, being together with each other, and being apart.

You may be with a spouse who is unable to exercise at the same level that you are, this may be a perfect opportunity to discuss what exercise you can participate in together and which activity you will do apart.

My husband has three stents in his heart so he is unable to run. We decided to walk each night after he gets home from work so we do some exercise together. I still felt I needed to exercise my body more, so I now get up early in the morning and go for my jog after he leaves for work. This way it is not affecting our time together and I am receiving the level of exercise my body needs.

I am now in the process of starting my personal morning exercise program that includes running and walking to get my stamina back. My goal is to be able to run 5 km without stopping. At age 60, this will be an excellent goal to meet.

I want you to think about what exercises you enjoy most. Do you prefer to do this activity alone or with your partner? I challenge you to set a start date to achieve your personal exercise goals. It's even more beneficial if you can tie your exercise to a social experience. Enjoy the social part of this activity and journal about how this practice, hopefully, a new-found habit, has helped you on your healing journey. I know this was one of the best steps I took in my forgiveness and healing journey. I started to take care of my body, which in turn helped me physically and emotionally.

Let's pray:
Heavenly Father we come to You today asking for You to give us the strength to move on from past hurts and trauma so we can start having the energy to get up in the morning, face our day and exercise our body and soul. We acknowledge that a huge part of our healing will be stepping out to take care of our bodies. We know that a healthy body will allow us to have the energy to fulfill the purpose You set out before us- whatever that may be. When we begin the step of exercising our body and socializing, we ask You to show us the people You would like us to communicate with and establish friendships with. We ask this in Jesus' name, and we pray. Amen

Reflections and steps to complete
Step 11

1) Decide on an exercise that you want to begin and begin your exercise journey with a goal in mind.

2) After you start your exercise program, record how you felt after each daily exercise. How did you feel about achieving your goal?

Group discussion or personal reflection

You may want to share your answers within your bible study or small group.

After reading the Bible verses in this chapter, which verse spoke to you the most about exercise and socialization?

1) *Do you not know that your body is a temple of the Holy Spirit, who is in you, whom you have received from God? You are not your own; You are not your own; you were bought at a price. Therefore honor God with your body.--1 Corinthians 6:19-20(NIV)*

2) *Therefore encourage one another and build each other up, just as in fact you are doing. --1 Thessalonians 5:11(NIV)*

You have now completed the tenth step of your healing process. Be proud of yourself. Pray to God whom He would like you to be vulnerable in sharing your exercise and socializing goals to help keep you accountable.

CHAPTER 9 PEACE TO PURPOSE

But the Counselor, the Holy Spirit, whom the Father will send in my name, will teach you all things and will remind you of everything I have said to you. Peace I leave with you; my peace I give you. I do not give to you as the world gives. Do not let your hearts be troubled and do not be afraid.-- John 14:26-27(NIV).

The state of peace occurs when we arrive at a state of tranquility in the inner soul. There is no anguish, bitterness, or resentment in our being. This peaceful state can be a perfect time to get in touch with who we are, what we hope to accomplish in life, and what steps we are willing to take to achieve our desired goals.

In this peaceful state, we are safely wrapped in our Father's arms and the Holy Spirit deepens our connection with God. We see ourselves through the lens of God, and he is our comforter who brings us to a deeper understanding of who we are in Christ. Finding this new identity, the person we are in Christ is like having a new set of lenses with a sense of inner peace of who we are supposed to be on earth. No one can take it or tarnish it because we keep it polished with positive peaceful thoughts that God is with us. We are deeply in touch with God and are completely connected to God; there is no room for negativity because His peace transcends beyond our wildest expectations. We pray, and He directs us toward His purpose.

Stepping out again with peace does not mean that you will not encounter obstacles during your journey. The key to staying positive is to stop and push the "pause for patience" button when meeting opposing people. "Pause for patience" means to stop, listen, do not assume responsibility for other people. Realize it is not about you; it is about them. If they are being negative, remain calm. If they are criticizing you do not allow their attack to reflect your character. Usually, hostility and anger are the result of unresolved issues from their past. You have done all you can to deal with your past and have reached a very peaceful state, so try all you can to brush attacks off. Continue to pray; pray for tranquility and peace.

Max Lucado's story, "You Are Special" depicts this beautifully. Lucia, one of the wooden puppets does not allow the stars or dots of evaluation of others to stick to her body. Punchinello inquires of Eli, the wood carver, why the dots and stars do not stick to his friend Lucia. Eli tells Punchenello that Lucia doesn't care about what others think, she only cares about what he thinks and he thinks she is pretty special. Punchenello doesn't want the stickers to stick to him either. Eli gently reminds him that as soon as he doesn't care about what others think and focuses on what his maker thinks, the stars and dots won't stick. Punchenello left his maker believing he too was special and as soon as he did the dots began to fall to the ground.

As we increasingly search for meaning and purpose in our lives, we will come to terms with that very question. Who do we allow to evaluate us, the people of the world or God? Being in touch with our maker God, He will allow us to have a clearer focus on our purpose in life. Without God, we will tend to worry and allow others to control us with their words, or actions.

Our true purpose in life can be revealed through prayer; ask God to lead us. Asking for direction in the steps we take in life guides us toward His plan for us. Often, we allow our environmental circumstances to take over and fill us with negative thoughts of who we are, which causes us to veer off the path of God's destiny. The world's negative point of view has no place and is most often contrary to what God is telling you about who you are and what you should do. Our identities are in God's perception of us, and not how the world views us. By getting closer contact with God through prayer, we can find our path set out before us. Praying daily for direction is the first step in allowing God to direct our paths.

Many of us have mundane routines in which our lives have the same schedule. We do not step out to take new adventures for fear of failure. God wants to challenge our lives. He wants us to have no fears and be brave in our endeavours, and to be all He has designed us to be. What does this look like? How can we clearly define our destiny so there is no question that we are in line with his purpose for our lives?

The first step is being purposeful in our daily meditation, praying for direction, and being in a state of quietness with God so that we can listen to His whispers. This calm state allows a person to hear without a doubt what God asks us to be. The verse I use to bring me to this quiet place is: ***"Be still and know that I am God." --Psalms 46:10(NIV)***

I mentioned the peaceful place I retreated to, called Inthestillness Retreat. It is nestled in the woods on top of a hill overlooking the Bay of Fundy. I was fortunate and persistent enough to purchase a piece of property next to Inthestillness and I now have my own sanctuary, which overlooks the same view. I renovated and glammed up an old travel trailer, which allows my husband and I to often retreat and enjoy the peacefulness of this place.

In Chapter Two, I discussed creating a peaceful place in your home or you may find this peaceful place in nature like I did. I challenge you if you have completed the 30-day forgiveness journey to continue to have time that you meet and ask for direction from God in your sanctuary. This will help you find peace and purpose in your life.

One of the best-written books and one I mentioned briefly in one of the previous chapters is "The Purpose Driven Life" by Rick Warren. This study book allows for weeks of studying, praying, and asking God for guidance in your life. I enjoyed the small-group discussions so much that I completed two: one at home when I was in Riverview, NB and one when I was on my exchange with Australia. God is amazing and shows up in many ways if we allow him to guide us.

What causes us to stumble along the path of life? Sometimes our stubbornness gets in the way. We try so desperately to control our lives that if we just allowed God to take the wheel, we would be so much better off. I have a friend whose focus in life was to follow in her mother's shoes—to marry, have family, create, and have fun. Her focus was on finding a man. She did, more than one in fact, and each time experienced incredible emotional pain. Finally, she decided to focus her life's plan on God's plan for her life. She felt she messed up terribly making life decisions and that going forward she would follow God's plan. She let go and let God and as a result God filled the desires of her heart. She experienced the joy of being in God's will, gaining more than she could give, AND she now has a partner that offers more than she could have dreamed. So don't be afraid to let go and let God. A popular country song "Jesus Take the Wheel' reminds us of the importance of allowing God to direct us along the road called life, so we are aligned with his purpose.

I tried to think of my past dating relationships and the common thread within them. I must admit that I did not spend enough time on the onset of each with God. I automatically thought God placed these people in my life, and He may very well have. I thought it was for life, but did not realize that His plan was for a season. A season is necessary for the growth of both individuals. Looking back, I can now understand why the season occurred and what I learned from each relationship. I felt it would have been much easier for the pain of my heart not to endure the anguish of another relationship.

I found myself praying to God, asking Him to bring me to the Godly man he designed for me. I think in the past I prayed, and when someone entered my life, I assumed he was automatically the man. I now know the importance of having a Godly man like Todd in my life when I face trials such as we have because we draw on our Heavenly Father to help us through good and bad times.

I remember once sitting in a school parking lot after a relationship breakup, tears streaming down my face, and feeling I was not on the peaceful path God had intended for me. I felt my job was mundane, day after day, and going through the same procedure. I just felt that God was calling me to do more. I remember looking up towards the sky and crying out, "God is this all you have intended for my life?" Please guide me to your Purpose?" I entered the school and was asked to receive a call from our district head; she offered me a short-term position, working alongside another mentor. My job would be working within the realm of writing and assisting the transition for students in French Immersion to studying the rest of the year in English. I was almost finished my Masters in Advanced Literacy, so this was the perfect fit for me. I wanted to share my passion for writing and all that I learned to the students and the teachers I was so blessed to work with. I remember saying, "Thank you God for that immediate response. Psalm 34: 17 reminds us that God hears our cries of anguish, he listens to our plea, and we just need to call on Him.

In this position, I had the privileged of fostering the love of writing in young writers. Through this season, I learned a great deal about how our passion and God's purpose in our lives can be perceived as a threat to those around us. I would be on fire when working with teachers who wanted to create a classroom that provided young writers with tools to allow them to express their thoughts freely. Students were engaged, and I felt that I was where God wanted me to be.

However, we cannot control the world. Through this season, I noticed the worldly people around me growing jealous of my energy and enthusiasm as I shared students' writing. I found myself taming back my enthusiasm for my job, as I sensed that others were not as pleased with my passion. Although my part in the lives of these writers was only for a season, I was blessed to witness what it feels like to be where God wants you to be. It truly did not feel like work, but that I was where I belonged.

When this position came to an end I was sad and wondered "Why?" I found myself growing somewhat resentful of the friend who took on the position and the co-workers I walked alongside who posed as friends but facilitated my downfall. During that season, I enjoyed every opportunity to make the teacher's I worked with life easier by purchasing and providing them with the tools necessary to foster the love of writing through writers' workshop. By the end of my weeks of working with the teachers and students they were equipped to incorporate a program that provided the writer with a step- by- step independent writers program.

Students brainstormed their topic, had opportunity to provide feedback to other students, and actually evaluate their own piece of writing, as well as their peers. As confident writers they eagerly embraced writers' workshop because they were taking ownership of their writing. They knew what would make their piece of writing polished and they knew the next steps to achieve this quality piece. Even though I had observed my passion for writing being passed on to the new teachers and their students, my time had completed its season. I remember one student who was a reluctant writer coming up to me sharing how he now enjoys journaling his writing. I received my evaluation from the teachers I was blessed to work alongside as well as the students. I had to accept the fact that for whatever the reason, my season had come to an end but I could walk away knowing I gave my heart and soul to this position.

Unfortunately, I didn't realize how the actions of one particular boss took a toll on me. She would try to discredit me with every school I worked at so I felt my credibility among teachers diminished and even though I confronted her, things just did not change. The bitterness I felt towards this person started creeping through my job. I watched this coworker use her position to further bully me. Year after year, I was subject to workplace bullying, and as much as I wanted to make light of it, it came to a head when my father became ill and I could not keep up with the demands at work and take care of my sick dad. Through prayer, I finally gained enough courage to face the fact that I needed to reposition myself so I was not working directly under this particular boss as she was sucking out all the joy in my life I usually had as a teacher.

Through trials and hurts in life—and we will continue to have them throughout our life—we need to call on our Heavenly Father to intercede on our behalf. Through daily prayers, we can remain assured that God has a plan. I had to trust He had a plan through the bullying I was facing at work because it followed me throughout the final years of my teaching. I started to feel the strong affects that occur from being a product of work place bullying that happened in my life. We can continue to harbour anger as I did towards colleagues and others, but this bitterness was eating away at who God wanted me to be. I did not like who I was becoming.

It can take years as it did for me to wallow in resentment, but we need to get to a peaceful state with our Lord before we can fulfill His designed purpose for our lives. Are you ready to find peace and know that the Lord has a plan and purpose, even through all the trauma and hurt you have faced in your life? Ask Him and He will show you your purpose.

Let's pray:
Heavenly Father we come to You today asking for peace and purpose in our lives. We are on our healing journey and know that we have tried to do things with our strength. Today, we give our lives to You. We know that there is peace waiting for us when we draw closer to You. Help us to regularly set time aside in our peaceful place to listen to Your still small voice and be sure that decisions we make we are without a doubt in your perfect will. We ask for peace and purpose in Jesus' name. Amen.

Reflections and steps to complete

1) Pray for God's plan for your life and write down where God is leading you on your walk with Him.

2) Do you have peace with where God is leading you? Are there areas you need to continue to pray and wait on the Lord?

Group discussion or personal reflection
You may want to share your answers within your bible or a small group.

After reading the Bible verses in this chapter, which verse spoke to you the most about finding peace and purpose in your life?

1) *But the Counselor, the Holy Spirit, whom the Father will send in my name, will teach you all things and remind you of*

everything I have said to you. Peace I leave with you; my peace I give you. I do not give to you as the world gives. Do not let your hearts be troubled and do not be afraid. John 14:26-27(NIV)
2) Be still and know that I am God."Psalms 46:10(NIV)

You are now on a journey to find peace and purpose in life. Be proud of yourself. Pray to God, whom He would like you to be vulnerable in sharing your journey.

CHAPTER 10 LOVING YOURSELF AND OTHERS

Love is patient, love is kind. It does not envy, it does not boast, it is not proud. It is not rude, it is not self-seeking, it is not easily angered, it keeps no record of wrongs. Love does not delight in evil but rejoices with the truth. It always protects, always trusts, always hopes, always perseveres. Love never fails. But where there are prophecies, they will cease; where there are tongues, they will be stilled; where there is knowledge, it will pass away.-- 1 Corinthians 13:4-8(NIV)

I think most of you would agree that it is difficult to love the unlovable—those who purposefully create chaos and suffering. It is even difficult to love those who are simply unkind and do not show love and compassion. We might see their motives as being selfish. Therefore, we prefer to keep our distance from those who don't show love and kindness. But God calls us to love. He clearly states in the bible: **"But I tell you who hear me: Love your enemies, do good to those who hate you, bless those who curse you, pray for those who mistreat you." --Luke 6: 27-28(NIV).** In a case where a person is feeling emotionally or physically hurt by someone, it would be important to seek a qualified counselor to be guided to how to deal with this situation. There may be a time when it would be best to remove yourself whether it be physically or emotionally, so that you are not subject to this kind of hurt. The Bible also states, **Do not give to dogs what is sacred; do not throw your pearls to pigs. If you do, they may trample them under their feet, and then turn and tear you to pieces.-- Matthew 7:6(NIV)**

Some of us have a difficult time loving ourselves. We try to show love to others but we don't feel our love is reciprocated. A possible cause for this is because we do not love ourselves first. It is impossible to love someone else until we first love ourselves.

God has designed you and only you for a purpose. No one else is genetically formed like you. Your characteristics, hair, face, body, mind and soul from head to toe was crafted by your Maker. Your DNA is His perfect plan. Think of the intrinsic detail involved in the development of the egg and the sperm of human life. God designed every little detail of that process so no two humans are exactly alike. Even identical twins are crafted with different personalities to clearly emphasize that our true identity is yes indeed God's perfect plan.

I had to acknowledge before God that I was not living obediently in loving myself. Instead I was disobediently in not loving the person God made me to be. I had to begin to love who He created. Search deeply into your past and the reasons why you disobediently withhold loving yourself. The Bible states:

For you created my inmost being; you knit me together in my mother's womb. I praise you because I am fearfully and wonderfully made; your works are wonderful, I know that full well. My frame was not hidden from you when I was made in the secret place. When I was woven together in the depths of the earth, your eyes saw my unformed body. -- Psalm 139:13-16(NIV)

Remember to begin your journaling in thanksgiving for all the wonderful gifts God has given you. Gifts you can use to touch the lives of the people in your life and to be thankful for who He made you to be, a beautiful child of the King. Once you have developed a love for yourself as a creation of God, you can then begin to love those around you and in your community. Embrace yourself, the creation God brought into the world to serve, and find purpose, so you can begin planting seeds in the lives of others.

God calls us to look at our bodies as a creation of His perfect and Holy plan to be all we can be. The Bible states, **After all, no one ever hated his own body, but he feeds and cares for it, just as Christ does the church-- Ephesians 5:29(NIV).** We need to feed and take care of the body God gave us honouring His perfect and pleasing will for our lives. He wants us to be healthy in body, mind, and spirit.

I read a book years ago that prompted me to wake up and be thankful for what God equipped me with to do His will on earth. The book is called "Life Without Limits" by Nick Vujicic; the author shares an account of his life—a life of living without limbs. He does not have legs or arms, but this man lives a life full and pleasing to God. He is a public speaker who encourages others to face challenges in life through a positive lens.

This book changed my life, I could see how God used a man like Nick, who had every reason in the world to give up and pity himself, to encourage others to be all they can be. Wow! The power of God's spirit and strength in Nick is a testimony to living a life free to be all God has intended. He used Nick tremendously, but the key is that Nick was willing to look beyond the world's perceived limitations and use his circumstance to encourage others to be all they can be.

The book reminded me of what the Bible states:
For we are God's workmanship, created in Christ Jesus to do good works, which God prepared in advance for us to do. Ephesians 2:10 (NIV).

Imagine how difficult it would be to face a day without limbs—no arms or hands, no legs or feet. Most of us don't have this extreme challenge. Most of us easily stretch out of bed and face the day; a day God has so freely given to us to complete His purpose in the world. I do realize there are some who have health issues or financial circumstances that may hinder their ability to be all they can be in the world. Whatever your limitation ask God to reveal to you how you can be used in that circumstance for His glory. All He calls us to do is be all we can be to the world and the people around us. That is what God equipped us with and He has a plan for you. However, we first need to begin by loving who He made us to be. What is hindering you from loving the person God made you to be? God does not make mistakes and you are not a mistake. I want you to look in the mirror and say the following.

_____ (say your name).You are made by God.
There is only one_____ (say your name)
He made me with_____ hair (place color)
He made me with_____eye (place color)
He made my body_____ perfect in His own way.
He made my personality_____ (funny, serious, etc)
He made me with the ability to_____ (your abilities)
Thank you, God, for the person you made me to be.

This is one area of my life where I have always struggled, but I was reminded after attending women's conferences and my most recent marriage weekend, that I am not alone in this journey. Women and men all seem to need people in their lives to affirm who they are and unfortunately, if our spouse, parents, siblings, or children have a difficult time communicating this need for acceptance, our love bucket becomes empty. But eventually, we need to come to the terms that it is God and only God who can truly fill our love bucket.

Years ago Todd and I started a gratitude journal for each other. We started January 1st and ended the following year and gave it to each other for Christmas. Each night we would write one thing that we appreciate that day about each other. There were days it was difficult to think of one thing and those were usually the days we had an argument. But even on those days, I managed to think of one thing I was grateful for about Todd. It can be so important to focus on the positive attributes of our spouse rather than the negative. This is true with any relationship we are in. We have a tendency to assume the worst of a person, ourselves included, rather than the best of a person or situation. But the most important person today is you and you need to focus on who God made you to be.

Over the next week, I challenge you to ask someone dear to you to write ten things they like about you with a small explanation of why. Then, I want you to look in the mirror again for the second time and add those loving things that the person said about you thanking God for those qualities.

In order to love others we have to first love ourselves for who God made us to be. It is so easy to look at others and all they have, or the qualities we find endearing that we do not have, but what a slap in the face to God. He designed you, and it is as though we are saying to God you could have done a better job. He is not happy with these thoughts because He thinks He did a pretty good job creating YOU to fulfill His plan in the world.

Unfortunately, we can become a hindrance to God's perfect plan by wallowing in all the limiting beliefs of, "if I had," or "if this didn't happen to me". But the funny thing is God is saying I meant for that to happen so this would be a result and because you are so stubborn and not willing to accept my plan, you are becoming a stumbling block. God's will, will be done with or without you. But would it not be better if we accepted the things that came our way, knowing that this was God's plan? Then be able to say, "God I know you have equipped me to face this challenge, and I promise to continue to love you and myself in spite of this challenge that is before me."

I was at my girlfriend's yesterday and she handed me a piece of paper about the things she loves about me. She told me the list over the phone on my 60th birthday but today she gave it to me to read. So I open it up and looked over the words she used to describe me. I selected 10 qualities that I felt God might be pleased with because they were the most pleasing for me:

1. Loves God
2. Reads the Bible
3. Honest
4. Enjoys Learning
5. Helps Voluntarily
6. Loves Todd and His faith
7. Loves to Chat with Friends
8. Loves Being a Mother and Nana
9. Creative
10 Adventurer

There were many qualities she listed, and I was so thankful that she took the time to do this because I was a little hard on myself, especially the past year. I did not know how others perceived me. But I do love that I am a Christian who loves God with all my heart, and a big part of my life is being in fellowship with others who want to read the Bible and enjoy learning. I like being known for being honest, and I know that if anyone asked me to help, I would be there at the drop of a hat. I love my husband and he is a man of God. I woke up this morning, finding him reading a book on intimacy that we just got in the mail, and that warmed my heart that he was working on his part of our journey. I absolutely love chatting, with friends and just about anyone. I always saw myself as an introvert, but as I age, I love to learn from others and share our different perspectives on life. I love being a Mother and Nana; it warms my heart when I hear the little ones saying they want to come and visit. God gifted me with being able to interact with little ones and I bond so easily with them. He also equipped me with being creative and full of adventures. I believe Todd, too, has a creative nature and we work well together in making candles and working on building our deck in St. Martins. I am blessed to have a very capable man and to have lots of my own capabilities.

After reading over the list that your friend or close relative wrote about you, were there qualities that affirmed who you are as a daughter or son in Christ? Think about all the blessings and gifts God has freely given to you so you might in turn be used to be a blessing to others.

Let's pray:
Heavenly Father we come to You today asking You to forgive us for not loving ourselves the way You have loved us. Help us to accept our challenges in life by knowing You have a plan and purpose through these challenges so we can be all we can be for You. We ask You to help us find ten things that we love about ourselves and can use for Your Glory. We ask you to give us the courage to use all of our abilities and gifts in loving our family and people in our community. In Jesus' name. Amen.

Reflections and steps to complete
Step 12

1) After reading the list that your friend or family member wrote about you, select 10 qualities on the list that you feel would be pleasing to God and also make your heart dance. Add them to your list, and pray that God reveals how He can use these qualities for His purpose.

2) How can you show love for your family, neighbour, or community this week?

Group discussion or personal reflection

You may want to share your answers within your Bible study or small group.

After reading the Bible verses in this chapter, which verse spoke to you the most when dealing with loving yourself and others?

1) *Love is patient, love is kind. It does not envy, it does not boast, it is not proud. It is not rude, it is not self-seeking, it is not easily angered, it keeps no record of wrongs. Love does not delight in evil but rejoices with the truth. It always protects, always trusts, always hopes, always perseveres. Love never fails. But where there are prophecies, they will cease; where there are tongues, they will be stilled; where there is knowledge, it will pass away.-- 1 Corinthians 13:4-8(NIV)*

2) *"But I tell you who hear me: Love your enemies, do good to those who hate you, bless those who curse you, pray for those who mistreat you." --Luke 6: 27-28(NIV).*

3) *Do not give to dogs what is sacred; do not throw your pearls to pigs. If you do, they may trample them under their feet, and then turn and tear you to pieces.— Mathew 7:6(NIV)*

4) *For you created my inmost being; you knit me together in my mother's womb. I praise you because I am fearfully and wonderfully made; your works are wonderful, I know that full well. My frame was not hidden from you when I was made in the secret place. When I was woven together in the depths of the earth, your eyes saw my unformed body. -- Psalm 139:13-16(NIV)*

5) *After all, no one ever hated his own body, but he feeds and cares for it, just as Christ does the church— Ephesians 5:29(NIV).*

6) *For we are God's workmanship, created in Christ Jesus to do good works, which God prepared in advance for us to do. Ephesians 2:10 (NIV).*

You have now completed the twelfth step of being all you can be in your life. Be proud of yourself. Pray and ask God whom He would like you to be vulnerable in sharing the ten qualities that you love about yourself.

CHAPTER 11 TRIGGERS THAT CAUSE US TO FALL

My dear brothers take note of this: Everyone should be be quick to listen, slow to speak, and slow to become angry, for anger does not bring about the righteousness life that God desires. -- James 1:19(NIV)

We all have our triggers in life that remind us of past hurts and our response to these hurts can cause us to sin. (ie: responding with harsh words, bitterness and anger.) The important part as Christians is to admit we have sinned and fallen away from what God has intended for our life. Triggers have a way of testing whether we have truly forgiven. Sometimes, as humans, we fall short by responding not Christ-like when faced with life's hurts. We need to identify the person who hurt us and follow the steps to forgiveness. Eventually, our goal is to observe these triggers becoming less and less as we look upon the triggers as a reflection of an area in the other person's flawed life. It is important to not allow this negative behaviour to rob us of the joy God intends for us to have in our life. God calls us to respond with silence, first being slow to speak and slow to anger. This can be difficult if past hurts causes us to feel victimized again. At times, these triggers surprisingly haunt our every being and the slightest mention of an injustice previously experienced brings up the hurt wounds from the past and leads us to vent.

So how can we overcome the hurt from the past so that these triggers don't cause us to sin? James 1:19 provides us with all the answers on how to deal with situations where our triggers manifest. Our first step is to be quick to listen—hear the other person tell their side of the story. This takes a great deal of practice because we have to hear things we may not want to hear.

The second part is to be slow to speak and this is even more difficult because when they speak there may be areas where we want to say, "but" to defend our position. And most importantly we need to be slow to be angry. Even Jesus got angry and sometimes we are justified with this response, but it mustn't cause us to stumble.

Just recently on my journey to healing, I was thinking I had made great strides on my walk but was reminded by little triggers that caused me to step back, look inwardly, and allow past trauma to control my emotions. It was a two-day pity party that put my writing on forgiveness journey on hold. I had to think about that; did it actually put it on hold or did it provide the opportunity for me to realize I am human and will stumble? I had a setback and I had to write and name it for what it was. You will probably have setbacks on your journey as well and I am here to tell you it isn't where you want to stay. Setbacks may seem insurmountable: however, they may be necessary on your journey in order to come to terms with areas that still need to be molded and polished, so you can be all you can be.

In Chapter One, I mentioned I was hurt by a dear friend—one who I would go to from time to time. This hurt set me back, but it gave me a reason to write that day about the stumble I faced. When all is going well on our journey we will feel like we have it all together only to find out that we are still looking to the world to validate who we are. Once again, not relying solely on our maker, we go to our fellow fallen humans and unfortunately they are not always equipped to guide us. I got a clear picture of how tender-hearted I was when I started seeing things for what they truly were; I was very sensitive. Even my husband knowingly or unknowingly was doing things that caused me grief and irritation. I had to stop and say, "Really Lise-Marie! Do you think he is trying to trigger you or is the enemy trying to stifle your walk?" I had to name it for what it was and continue.

So instead of going to man, I decided I would go to scripture. I was reminded in the Bible scripture, **for it is God who works in you to will and to act according to his good purpose." Philippians 2:13(NIV).**

So there you have it. God allows circumstances to take place, good or bad, all according to His purpose. We do have the ability to control our circumstances, to some degree, with how we respond. I guess in some ways I wouldn't be able to write about this unless it happened to me.

One thing I am learning to do is to not dwell as long on triggers. If we look back on our life, are there things we wrote about in our journal that we thought were so huge at the time, but now kind of chuckle at thinking, "Why was I so upset?" So I had to remind myself that this too shall pass. In the big scheme of things, it is small and won't have any bearing on my life in a day or two.

We cannot allow our present circumstances to get in the way of who God has called us to be. I had to think about the little events that occurred where I allowed myself to ruminate. The enemy was having a field day—taking hold of my thoughts and causing bitterness and undue stress. I had to ask God to release any hostility or bitterness toward anyone and every day to search my heart on my healing journey. I asked for Him to allow me to forgive little infractions along the way so I could continue His will to my freedom to forgive. I certainly didn't want to prolong my healing journey. God wants a full renewal and I want what He has in store for my life.

Here is a psalm that I say daily before I begin my day so that God can reveal any bitterness in my heart:

Search me, O God, and know my heart; test me and know my anxious thoughts. See if there is any offensive way in me, and lead me in the way everlasting. Psalm 139:23-24(NIV)

If you ask God to reveal any thoughts that are not pleasing to Him He will reveal this to you, because God wants you to be all you can be. Sometimes it takes time alone to pray, but not just pray, to listen to what God is saying and calling you to do.

You will probably, like me, have triggers that remind you that you truly haven't forgiven certain people in your life. For example: if I am constantly rehashing an incident with someone, that's a sign I haven't forgiven and I need to take action. I would then revisit the steps to forgiveness by recognizing the hurt and writing detail-by-detail about the hurt. Write a letter and either send or burn the letter; stay in prayer to listen to what God is calling you to do.

Don't be too hard on yourself when triggers happen. Ask God to reveal what he wants you to do with the trigger. Write down what your next steps will be and realize forgiveness is a lifelong journey. I realized that forgiveness is an ongoing practice, and sometimes when we have gone through the above process and felt we forgave, later in life we are reminded that our forgiving was not fully completed. You may have encounters like I did.

A couple of years ago I was chatting with someone dear to me about a legal case involving a taxi cab driver and an intoxicated female victim of rape. The cab driver was being accused of rape by the female passenger. He had picked her up and was suppose to bring her safely home but instead pulled over on the side of the road and said he had consensual sex with this intoxicated female passenger. My response to him defending the judge who acquitted the taxi cab driver was one of rage and anger.

As I drove home chatting to my husband on the phone, fuming about the conversation I had with this person, I realized this situation was so personal to me. I wanted to seek justice for this woman who was wrongly accused of being an intoxicated drunk who, as the judge claimed, could have consented to the taxi driver having sex with her. The old war wounds of shame of my past encounter at university during my frosh week reared its ugly head and I wanted to be sure justice prevailed. Make no mistake, my response was not one of forgiveness—but more like revenge.

But anger is not something one should repress, but express to get through the pain of past events. We have to acknowledge the triggers that cause old wounds to surface and begin again in our forgiveness journey. I mentioned the steps I took to free myself from the bondage of unforgiveness. If you have gone through the steps and continue to have resentment it might be beneficial to take your forgiveness one step further. Just as Alcoholics Anonymous has 12 steps to recovery I too believe these steps can be used to assist in our forgiveness, our mistrust, shame, and any areas in our life we have difficulty.

12 steps

1. Admit we were powerless over the effects of our separation from God- that our lives have become unmanageable. I know nothing good lives in me, that is, in my sinful nature. For I have the desire to do what is good, but I cannot carry it out. (Romans 7:18)

2. Come to believe that a power greater than ourselves can restore us to sanity. For it is God who works in you to will and to act according to His good purpose (Phi. 2:13)

3. Make a decision to turn our will and our lives over to the care of God as we understand Him.

Therefore, I urge you, brothers, in view of God's mercy, to offer your bodies as living sacrifices, holy and pleasing to God- which is your spiritual worship. (Romans 12:1)

4. Make a searching and fearless inventory of ourselves.

Let us examine our ways and test them, and let us return to the Lord (Lam. 3:40)

5. Admit to God, to ourselves, and to another human being the exact nature of our wrongs.

Therefore confess your sins to each other and pray for each other so that you may be healed. (James 5:16)

6. We are entirely ready to have God remove all these defects of character.

Humble yourselves before the Lord, and He will lift you up (James 4:10

7. Humbly ask Him to remove our shortcomings.

If we confess our sins, He is faithful and just and will forgive us our sins and purify us from all unrighteousness (1 John 1:9)

8. Make a list of all persons we had harmed and become willing to make amends to them all.

Do to others as you would have them do to you. (Luke 6:31)

9. Make direct amends to such people wherever possible except when doing so would injure them or others.

Therefore, if you are offering your gift at the altar and there remember that your brother has something against you, leave your gift there in front of the altar. First, go and be reconciled to your brother; then come and offer your gift. (Matt. 5:23-24)

10. Continue to take a personal inventory, and when we are wrong, promptly admit it.

So, if you think you are standing firm, be careful that you don't fall. (1 Cor. 10:12)

11. Sought through prayer and meditation to improve our conscious contact with God as we understand Him praying only for knowledge of His will for us and the power to carry that out.

Let the word of Christ dwell in you richly. (Col. 3:16)

12. Having a spiritual awakening as the result of these steps, we then try to carry this message to others and practice these principles in all our affairs.
Brothers, if someone is caught in a sin, you who are spiritual should restore him gently. But watch yourself, or you also may be tempted. (Gal. 6:11)

I pray that after deeply going through the above steps you felt a sense of healing and peace. Forgiveness is not an easy road but one, if done with surrender to God, can provide an overwhelming sense of peace.

Let's pray:
Heavenly Father we come to You today with ongoing past hurts that surface and are causing us to stumble. We are aware that triggers are going to happen in our life, but we need Your power to help us to respond in a Christ-like and loving way. We ask that You free us once and for all from the bondage of an unforgiving heart. We name the incident_____ and person_____ that has caused a trigger and we ask for your healing power to release us of the bondage this trigger has held in our life. Please help us to break free of any sin in our life that is causing us to respond in an unloving way. Help us to respond in a loving way even when we feel we are being attacked. Forgive us for our shortcomings when we do not respond in a Christ-like way. We ask for healing in Jesus' name. Amen.

Reflections and steps to complete
Step 13

1) Name the trigger and your response to the trigger.

2) Complete the 12 steps to recovery listed in this chapter.

Group discussion or personal reflection
You may want to share your answers within your Bible study or small group.

After reading the Bible verses in this chapter, which verse spoke to you the most when dealing with healing and triggers?

1) My dear brothers take note of this: Everyone should be be quick to listen, slow to speak, and slow to become angry, for anger does not bring about the righteousness life that God desires. --James 1:19(NIV)

2) for it is God who works in you to will and to act according to his good purpose." Philippians 2:13(NIV).

3) Search me, O God, and know my heart; test me and know my anxious thoughts. See if there is any offensive way in me, and lead me in the way everlasting.—Psalm 139:23-24(NIV)

4) Or any Scriptures that spoke to you in the 12-step recovery listed above

You have now completed the thirteenth step in forgiving and healing the hurts in your life. Be proud of yourself. Pray and ask God whom He would like you to be vulnerable in sharing your steps to healing with.

CHAPTER 12 PROMISES ARE YES IN CHRIST

For no matter how many promises God has made, they are "Yes" in Christ. And so through him, the "Amen" is spoken by us to the glory of God. Now it is God who makes both us and you stand firm in Christ. He anointed us, set his seal of ownership on us, and put his Spirit in our hearts as a deposit, guaranteeing what is to come.—2 Corinthians 1: 20-22(NIV)

Do not conform any longer to the pattern of this world, but be transformed by the renewing of your mind. Then you will be able to test and approve what God's will is- his good, pleasing, and perfect will. Romans 12:2(NIV)

I mentioned earlier that I attended a retreat in New York and felt blessed to be a part of such a faith-filled room full of believers. I remember mentioning to my husband that African Americans have such a powerful worship. *2 Corinthians 1: 20-22,* written above, speaks of the power of their worship. They live in the faith of knowing God will fulfill His promises. They stand firm as a body in Christ believers preaching confidently that God's YES will indeed fulfill His promises to those who stand firm and believe. His promises are true.

I stood in awe at the conference admiring their bold preaching as they spoke of His promises and powerfully ending each with a strong Amen; they know His promises will be a definite YES in being accomplished for God's glory. The confidence we lack is, not understanding the strength God uses to fulfill His purpose in the world through us. Once again as Christian believers, we unite together believing nothing is too difficult for our Lord to accomplish in us if we stand firm in the belief that God is the Father of miracles. I remember one Pastor speaking boldly to the women in the crowd, prophesying what God revealed to her about them.

I listened intently as she pointed to one woman who she said would be working in government, and it just so happened she was studying to do just that and the Pastor revealed that she could see her behind a desk at the White House being a powerful influence in her position. She went on to point to another woman to say she would be married to a pastor who would want to control her, but she was to stand up for who God had intended her to be for His glory. When she came over my way, as I mentioned in a past chapter, I tried to see if she was speaking to someone near me but her eyes went directly to mine and she said you will influence a million people. She went on and then later came over and said it again; you will influence a million people. I was overwhelmed with this news and I went to my room and tears started streaming down my face. I asked God just how He planned to accomplish that in me. It then occurred to me at that moment that I was to be used by writing this book. I always felt He was calling me to write but on that day it became evident through Him speaking through the Pastor.

So here I sit writing my final chapter of this book in the hopes in some small way this book has impacted your walk with the Lord. I can honestly say He guided me with each word that crossed every page. It is not a coincidence you are reading my story and the lives of those who crossed my path.

There are no shortcuts to the freedom of forgiveness. Your walk with God is the most important part of your life. Remember to let go and let God deal with your hurts. If you fail to complete the healing process and still find it difficult to go to the cross, know that you are not ready for healing. This too is okay, it just means you need more time to heal and wrap yourself in your loving father's arms. Don't rush the process; God will let you know when it is time to come out of the cocoon. You may be there for months—as I was. My grandchildren gave me a blanket that was hugged by them. I cried at this beautiful gift, and a note from them that read;

Nana
We hugged this blanket
We squeezed it really tight
We filled it with our wishes
Hope and love and light
So when you are feeling low
You will feel our love within it
Just hold it really tight
Morning, noon, and night.

I use this blanket every day and night when I am feeling low and need the warmth of the hugs of my precious grandchildren on my healing journey. It was the cocoon of those precious hugs, along with God's loving arms wrapped around me that helped me feel safe and secure. I knew I wasn't ready to forgive yet and no one will be able to tell you when your time to forgive will be. Allow yourself the freedom to feel the bitterness, anger, sadness, and emotion that came from the traumatic event that occurred. You aren't ready and that is okay. Pamper yourself and allow yourself the freedom to cry and be okay with that. Call only trusted people that will be there on your journey. You will know who God presents that can be there for you. You will have to say goodbye for a time to anyone who compromises your healing time and tries to rush you along.

God bless you for taking this journey to forgiveness. I will pray for you that the words in this book that God brought to me to share with you, will bring comfort in knowing you are not alone even when at times it feels like it. God is there and He will help you heal your deepest wounds so you can live free, freely forgiving so you can be a blessing to all those people whose path you will cross in this great journey called life. You too have a purpose; you are unique and God has a perfect plan for your life. Now "fear not" and "Go" where God leads you. Enjoy the ups and downs of your journey with God, knowing your life is mapped out and He will use uniquely you to glorify His holy name. Amen.

Let's pray:
Heavenly Father we come to You today with thanksgiving for all You have done on our journey to forgiveness. You have helped us to heal deep wounds and we feel the strength in knowing you will be with us through the next chapters we face in life. Help us to continue to be faithful in further developing our relationship with You and going to Your word daily for guidance in our next steps in life. We are in awe of what You have done for us and eagerly wait in anticipation of how You will use us for Your glory in the future. We ask for continuous healing and protection in Jesus' name. Amen.

Reflections and steps to complete
Step 14

1) Once I found peace, I started to pray and ask God how He could use me in my community or church to serve him. It is important to connect with people and have a sense of purpose. Where can God use you in your church or community?

2) What promise do you believe God will faithfully accomplish through you?

Group discussion or personal reflection
You may want to share your answers within your Bible study or small group.

After reading the Bible verses in this chapter, which verse spoke to you the most? Explain.

1) *For no matter how many promises God has made, they are "Yes" in Christ. And so through him, the "Amen" is spoken by us to the glory of God. Now it is God who makes both us and you stand firm in Christ. He anointed us set his seal of ownership on us, and put his Spirit in our hearts as a deposit, guaranteeing what is to come.—2 Corinthians 1: 20-22(NIV)*

2) *Do not conform any longer to the pattern of this world, but be transformed by the renewing of your mind. Then you will be able to test and approve what God's will is- his good, pleasing, and perfect will. Romans 12:2(NIV)*

You have now completed the fourteenth and final step in finding peace and purpose through the hurts in your life. Be proud of yourself. Pray and ask God whom He would like you to be vulnerable with in sharing your next steps.

RESOURCES

Chapter 1: The Hurt
1. Scripture taken from the *Holy Bible, New International Version®*. Copyright © 1973,1978,1984, By International Bible Society. Used in permission of Zondervan. All rights reserved.

Chapter 2: Peaceful Place
1. Scripture taken from the *Holy Bible, New International Version®*.Copyright © 1973,1978,1984, By International Bible Society. Used in permission of Zondervan. All rights reserved.
2. https://providentfilms.org/movies/war-room/
3. https://www.inthestillness.net/

Chapter 3: The Letters
1. Scripture taken from the *Holy Bible, New International Version®*. Copyright © 1973,1978,1984, By International Bible Society. Used in permission of Zondervan. All rights reserved.
2. https://utmost.org/

Chapter 4: Healing
1. Scripture taken from the *Holy Bible, New International Version®*. Copyright © 1973,1978,1984, By International Bible Society. Used in permission of Zondervan. All rights reserved.
2. https://www.justwatch.com/ca/movie/what-about-bob
3. https://www.livinginfreedom.ca/
4. https://intimacyanorexia.com/
5. https://www.familylifecanada.com/weekend-getaway-marriage-conferences/

Chapter 5: The Truth
1. Scripture taken from the *Holy Bible, New International Version®*. Copyright © 1973,1978,1984, By International Bible Society. Used in permission of Zondervan. All rights reserved.
2. https://www.focusonthefamily.ca/get-help/counselling#:~:text=Request%20to%20speak%20with%20a,speak%20with%20the%20care%20associate.

Chapter 6: Betrayal
1. Scripture taken from the *Holy Bible, New International Version®*. Copyright © 1973,1978,1984, By International Bible Society. Used in permission of Zondervan. All rights reserved.
2. Bennett, William J. *"Someone Sees You."pg.68. Children's Book of Virtues.* : Simon & Schuster, 1995

Chapter 7: Go! Fear Not
1. Scripture taken from the *Holy Bible, New International Version®*. Copyright © 1973,1978,1984, By International Bible Society. Used in permission of Zondervan. All rights reserved.
2. Warren, Rick. *Purpose Driven Life. United States: Zondervan, 2002*
3. Taking off the Mask - 2019 Women's Conference (July 19th & July 20th)- Free is Friday at 3:30 PM Organized by *I Am My Sister (Women helping Women) Ministry*
4. https://macleans.ca/news/canada/untold-story-justin-bourque/

Chapter 8: Exercise and Socialize
1. Scripture taken from the *Holy Bible, New International Version®*. Copyright © 1973,1978, 1984, By International Bible Society. Used in permission of Zondervan. All rights reserved.

Chapter 9: Peace and Purpose
1. Scripture taken from the *Holy Bible, New International Version®*. Copyright © 1973,1978, 1984, By International Bible Society. Used in

permission of Zondervan. All rights reserved.

2. Lucado, Max. *You Are Special.* Crossway Books, 1997.
3. Warren, Rick. *Purpose Driven Life.* United States: Zondervan, 2002

Chapter 10: Loving Yourself and Others
1. Scripture taken from the *Holy Bible, New International Version®.* Copyright © 1973, 1978, 1984, By International Bible Society. Used in permission of Zondervan. All rights reserved.
2. Vujicic, Nick. *Life Without Limits. NewYork:* Crown Publishing Group, 2010.

Chapter 11: Triggers That Cause Us To Fall
1. Scripture taken from the *Holy Bible, New International Version®.* Copyright © 1973, 1978, 1984, By International Bible Society. Used in permission of Zondervan. All rights reserved.
2. https://www.celebraterecovery.com/resources/12-steps

Chapter 12: Promises Are Yes In Christ

1. Scripture taken from the *Holy Bible, New International Version®.* Copyright © 1973, 1978, 1984, By International Bible Society. Used in permission of Zondervan. All rights reserved.
2. Taking off the Mask - 2019 Women's Conference (July 19th & July 20th)- Free is Friday at 3:30 PM Organized by *I Am My Sister (Women helping Women) Ministry*
3. https://www.etsy.com/ca/search?q=we%20hugged%20this%20blanket&ref=search_bar

www.ingramcontent.com/pod-product-compliance
Lightning Source LLC
Chambersburg PA
CBHW070614050426
42450CB00011B/3052